The Raindrops on the Windshield Sound Like Popcorn

The Raindrops on the Windshield Sound Like Popcorn

Colleen Sullivan Clapper

WinePress WP Publishing

WinePress Publishing (PO Box 428, Enumclaw, WA 98022) functions only as book publisher. As such, the ultimate design, content, editorial accuracy, and views expressed or implied in this work are those of the author.

Unless otherwise noted, all Scriptures are taken from the *Holy Bible, New International Version*®, *NIV*®. Copyright © 1973, 1978, 1984 by the International Bible Society. Used by permission of Zondervan. All rights reserved.

Scripture references marked AMP are taken from *The Amplified Bible, Old Testament*, © 1965 and 1987 by The Zondervan Corporation, and from *The Amplified New Testament*, © 1954, 1958, 1987 by The Lockman Foundation. Used by permission.

Scripture references marked KJV are taken from the *King James Version* of the Bible.

Scripture references marked NKJV are taken from the *New King James Version*, © 1979, 1980, 1982 by Thomas Nelson, Inc., Publishers. Used by permission.

ISBN 13: 978-1-57921-971-0
ISBN 10: 1-57921-971-3
Library of Congress Catalog Card Number: 2008929180

This book is dedicated to my children: James, Joshua and Jessica. I hope you always experience raindrops that sound like popcorn and see the promises of His rainbows. I pray that you may always know the love of God. He loves you even more than I do . . . which is incomprehensible!

"For He shall give His angels charge over you."

—Psalm 91:11, NKJV

Contents

Acknowledgments

This book has been years in the making. It has been a difficult project, and the end result is my being as real and raw as I can be. It has required the encouragement, input, editing and prayer support of people too numerous to mention all by name. A heartfelt thanks goes out to each one of you.

Introduction
The Raindrops on the Windshield
Sound Like Popcorn

Why the crazy title?

It was raining—somewhere between a torrential downpour and a spring shower. It was the kind of storm that made coming up with a strategy to cross a parking lot with a three-month-old, a two-year-old, a stroller, an umbrella and a diaper bag just beyond my mental capacity at that moment. I was attempting to run errands, and as I tried to devise a creative plan, my mind was blank. I've heard it referred to as "motherhood amnesia"—a common condition among moms due to sleep deprivation and a daily overdose of one purple, singing dinosaur.

My mind wandered . . . the pelting rain . . . an image of Hawaii . . . a transient sprinkle on a white sandy beach. The cloud passed, and the sun shone warm on my face. I felt the sand between my toes as I stepped into the crystal blue water . . . .

"Mom!"

I was jolted back to reality.

"The raindrops on the windshield sound like popcorn," Jimmie exclaimed from the back seat.

A favorite piece of encouragement I give new parents is that from the very moment they find out they're having a baby, there will not be a day without a smile. (Even if it's a day where you lock yourself in a bathroom and scream, you will smile when they are asleep.) How wonderful it is to think and reason as innocently as a child. How sad it is that, as adults, our worldly knowledge discourages simple thoughts, simple pleasures, and the ability to see miracles happening constantly all around us.

I've already explained the reason for the popcorn in the title, but what about the rainbow on the cover? In this world where most people have stopped looking for miracles, I have always found hope by looking at rainbows. For me, they are not just the things of fairy tales or pots of gold, but very real, physical reminders of God's presence in my life.

He has repeatedly proven Himself near to me in my trials and in control of the circumstances of my life. I have experienced the death of a child, a sabotaged adoption, a life-threatening illness, a fatal family accident, and hundreds of thousands of dollars of medical debt. If you had told me ahead of time that such trials were coming my way, I would have told you I could not have made it through them all. But through these trials, which I detail in the following chapters, God was always there. He was there when I worked in the prison and saw what survival means through the life of a young torture victim. He was there through four difficult pregnancies and, in Hollywood, He showed me that having Him is having everything. His grace through the adversities has been more than sufficient.

It takes both sun and rain to make a rainbow. To take it a step further, it is the Son, Jesus Christ, being the light through the hard times that creates a spectrum of hope, love, joy, peace, faith and blessing in our lives. The colors have been brilliant, and I have been truly blessed. These are the reasons why I have written this book—to encourage you to hear popcorn in the raindrops and to see amazing rainbows.

Chapter 1

Butterflies and Rainbows

He was gorgeous. He had amazing brown eyes, with hair to match, a chiseled chin and a lean build. As my friends and I washed cars that day to raise funds for high school dance camp, he walked up to me and he struck up a conversation. It required little effort from either of us. His smile, coupled with his casual attitude, was disarming. His name was Pat. He asked if we could get together sometime. Spontaneity was my preferred mode of operating, so I agreed to meet him later that night.

We met at my house with some other friends, and Pat and I talked for hours. He was friendly and confident, but not in an arrogant way. When he left, he kissed me on the cheek, promising to call. He called the next day, and the day after that. We went out on a few dates and had a great time. He was always a gentleman. I found out through mutual friends that he had been popular in school but had a reputation for partying in excess at times. I kept Pat at a friendly distance and, by doing so, he stopped calling.

The following summer, I went out with friends one night. We drove with the windows down and the radio blasting '80s tunes. We stopped at a convenience shop to get some drinks, and there was Pat. He looked as cute as ever, and he was extremely friendly. He and his friends invited us over, so my two girlfriends and I thought it over (briefly) and agreed. We followed them a few blocks to his friend's apartment. There, we listened to music and talked for a while.

I had on a white tank top with wide straps and a peach palm tree on the front and peach walking shorts (it was the '80s!). I wouldn't have even remembered what I wore, except that extensive reflection on the events that followed forced me to do so.

Before long, Pat said he had something to tell me and asked me to follow him into the other room. I brushed off a faint internal warning by rationalizing to myself that we were just going to talk.

Once in the room, Pat pulled me toward him hard and began kissing me aggressively. I resisted as his five o'clock shadow scraped my face. My eyes darted back and forth, and my stomach did flip-flops. I tried to pull away from him, but his grasp was too tight. This could not be happening to me. Not with someone I knew. Not with my friends just down the hallway. How? Why?

One of Pat's friends pounded on the door afterward. His friend seemed to sense that something was very wrong. Pat walked out the door, and I composed myself the best I could. His friend had a look of apologetic sadness on his face. I looked away and hurried to the bathroom where I wiped the mascara from my wet cheeks and fixed myself up. I asked my friends if we could leave. On the way home, they asked why I was so quiet. All I could tell them was, "I'm just tired."

I took a bath when I got home, but I couldn't scrub hard enough to make myself feel clean. Afterward, as I sat on the floor next to my bed, I was aware of every scrape and bruise. But the pain went much deeper than that. As I grasped my knees close to my body, an unfamiliar weakness engulfed me. Tears streamed down my face, and pain overtook me.

Through the fog, I began searching for answers. I remembered an English teacher in high school who had introduced me to existentialism. She'd given me books by Frankyl, Conrad and Richard Bach, and from them I had learned that things only happened if and because I wanted them to. Even though this was contrary to the belief system with which I'd been brought up, I began to rationalize that a mixture of Christianity and New Age better suited me. This led me to conclude that I must have wanted to be hurt—that I'd asked for it—or it wouldn't have happened.

The next day, Pat's friend called to tell me that Pat had been in a motorcycle accident and was slightly bruised but had no serious injuries. He had been doing cocaine all night, which, in all honesty, I hadn't known about or even suspected. I was silent. I eventually thanked him for the call, and then hung up.

When Pat called a few hours later, I assumed he was going to apologize. I was shocked when he asked if I wanted to go out again. I wanted to scream, but the words froze in my throat. With my hand shaking, I hung up the phone, and we never spoke again. I did see him a few years later at a mall. I had envisioned scenarios of a chance meeting like this and of getting some kind of verbal revenge, but I froze again. He saw me and, as recognition sparked in his eye, he just stared and smiled. I turned away, repulsed.

The anger I felt for Pat has since been replaced by pity. I wish I knew then what I know now—that I could have and should have pursued professional help. I thought about telling the police at one point, but I was afraid they would not believe me. It seemed these thoughts were validated when my mom, who didn't know the whole story, took me to a gynecologist who told me that what I had experienced was a "normal" first-time.

I was so confused, and I felt filthy. I hid this secret and was determined to bury it. I would live up to the expectations I thought others had of me. During my senior year, my peers nominated me as "Most Likely to Succeed," and I won "Most Friendly." I was thankful that people identified me that way, but I placed pressure on myself to live up to what I perceived were their expectations of me.

I headed off to college and was ready to "succeed." Things seemed to be falling into place. And yet, I felt burdened with a great loneliness. I kept the pain inside. I didn't even tell my closest friends for years. In addition, I just could not escape the feeling that I had let God down and that He was disappointed with me.

Maybe it was due to late nights of studying and hanging out with friends, eating beer nuggets (a Northern Illinois University staple) or the budget-friendly bologna sandwiches, or maybe it was the stress, but I ended up with appendicitis. My parents, who had received a call from the college medical clinic, drove 30 miles to the hospital ER.

They arrived just as I was being rushed to the operating room on the suspicion that my appendix had begun to burst. That diagnosis turned out to be correct, and I had an appendectomy.

During my recovery, I developed an allergic reaction to some of my prescriptions. So, my healing process was prolonged as much by the drugs as by the toxic combination of self-reliance and self-condemnation that was poisoning my mind and spirit. Even though I remained outwardly outgoing and friendly, I was slowly dying on the inside.

Within weeks, I dropped out of college.

Again, I wondered if I had actually wanted this. My newly created belief system told me that I might have subconsciously willed this into reality. According to existentialism, we control our surroundings and circumstances, but that whole thought process seemed to produce in me more chaos than peace. I struggled even more with my relationship with God.

Back home, I decided to attend a party given by my high school friends. It was great seeing everyone again. As the night went on, I began listening to people's problems. For some reason, people like to tell me their problems and ask me for advice. I really don't mind it. I enjoy helping others, but that particular night, their problems seemed to compound my own. I drank beer and, in hindsight, realized that I should never have been drinking with the various medications I was taking. I continued to laugh, smile, listen and counsel people, but my loneliness grew. I wanted to tell someone how much I was hurting, but I didn't.

I got sick that night and ended up back in the hospital. Because I was 18, I was still considered pediatric, but the hospital didn't have any room on the children's floor. Instead, they wheeled me to the adult floor and into a semi-private room. All I wanted to do was sleep, but before I even made it out of the wheelchair, a woman pulled the curtain back exclaiming, "I want to see who my new roommate is!"

Her name was Alma, and even in my condition her exuberance was contagious. She was beautiful. She was a little less than five feet tall, with coco brown skin, and had a mischievous smile that made everyone want to know what she was up to. Alma was a wife, a mother, and someone who became my friend.

For the next half hour, she showered me with question after question. Wanting to be polite, I answered each of them. Eventually, a nurse came to get her for treatment. I later learned that she was suffering from cancer and multiple sclerosis and that the treatments were mainly an attempt to ease her pain. I am convinced that our sharing a room was a "divine appointment."

My friendship with Alma was effortless and seemed to come naturally. We both loved art. She loved butterflies, and I loved rainbows. We were one heck of a match. We laughed so much that we got in trouble from the nurses for not getting enough rest. They learned that scolding us was a losing battle and always left our room in better spirits, smiling and shaking their heads.

Alma's family was also amazing. The first time we met, they invited me to join them in prayer. I was not used to people praying out loud in a circle while holding hands, but I was up for something new. I was so comforted as I listened to their prayers and saw their love for God. Their joy eclipsed their pain and worry.

A few nights later, I heard Alma crying. She was in terrible pain. Her IV had come out, and the constant drip of pain medication had ceased supplying her with much-needed relief. The nurses and doctors were all attending to a man who had suffered a heart attack and were not responding to Alma's call button.

I got out of bed. The floor was cold under my bare feet and my body ached, but I knew my pain was nothing compared to the pain Alma was experiencing. I walked slowly over to her bedside and found her hand. As I held it in mine, I felt the most amazing peace warm me and ease my fears. I felt God's touch. I sensed Jesus in her, and in the squeeze of her hand I experienced the unconditional love that I had heard He had for each of us. I had gone to her to ease her pain, but to my surprise God had used her to heal mine. As her tears began to cease, mine began to fall. I felt His love that night in a hospital room.

A few days later, I was discharged from the hospital. I promised to keep in touch with Alma and called her at home a couple of weeks later, only to find out that she was no longer in pain. My friend was gone, but I had no doubt where she was. She went to see Him face to face.

I often see butterflies and rainbows together and think of Alma. She gave me such special insight into God's love. I felt a renewed lease on life. I wanted to see what He had in store for me. Alma had unbelievable joy during such a dark time in her life. She was still able to laugh in spite of her circumstances. I wanted the same for my life. Little did I know at the time how much I would need it in the future.

When I was 13, my mom wrote me a letter in which she said that the enemy, the devil, would tempt me because I wanted to follow God. I believe the enemy did try (and has repeatedly tried) to stop my life. It is his mission to kill and destroy. Being a master of deception, he wanted me to believe that I did not deserve the love of God. Alma helped me discover what a lie that was. I renewed my resolve to follow God.

Jesus was in Gethsemane the night before He was crucified. He knew He was going to experience hatred and death. The anxiety He was feeling even caused Him to sweat drops of blood. Yet He knew that He had to go through those experiences and conquer them so you could have the opportunity for eternal life. God cares about you so much that He gave His only son to die for you. I can tell you that I believe with all my heart that no matter what you have done or not done—no matter how you've sinned or what guilt you're carrying—you're still welcome to sit at God's "dinner" table.

> Come to me, all you who are weary and burdened, and I will give you rest.
>
> —Matthew 11:28

Meeting My Husband

Everyone longs to give themselves completely to someone, to have a deep soul relationship with another, and to be loved thoroughly and exclusively. But, God says: "Not until you are satisfied, fulfilled, and content with being loved by Me alone; with giving yourself totally and unreservedly to Me; to having an intensely personal and unique relationship with Me alone, and discovering that only in Me is your satisfaction to be found; will you then be capable of the perfect human relationship that I have planned for you. You will never be united with another until you are united with Me—exclusive of anyone or anything else, exclusive of any other desires or longings.

I want you to stop planning and wishing and allow Me to give you the most thrilling plan existing, one that you cannot imagine! I want you to have the best. Please allow Me to bring it to you. You just keep watching Me, expecting the greatest things; to keep experiencing the satisfaction that I AM. Keep listening and learning the things I tell you. You just wait, that's all. Don't be anxious. Don't worry. Don't look around at the things others have gotten or that I've given them. Don't look at the things you think you want. You just keep looking off far and away, up to ME, or you'll miss what I want to show you. And then, when you're ready, I'll surprise you with a love far more wonderful than even you would dream of.

You see, until you are ready (I am working even at this moment to have both of you ready at the same time), until you are both satisfied exclusively with Me and the life I have prepared for you, you will not be able to experience the love that exemplifies your relationship with Me, and thus the 'perfect love.' And dear one, I want you to have this beautiful love. I want to see in the flesh a picture of your relationship with Me and to enjoy materially and concretely the everlasting union of beauty, perfection and love that I offer you with Myself. Know that I love you totally. Believe it and be satisfied."

—Author unknown

As many young girls do, I dreamt of my wedding day and even made a list of the qualities I thought were important in a good husband. I prayed for him and would often think about how he was out there somewhere. I came to realize that God would meet my expectations and go beyond what I had dared to dream. If marriage is in God's plans for you, His desire is for you to have a mate that will help fulfill His purposes in your life.

After recovering at home from the appendectomy, I felt well enough to visit my friend Missy, who took classes at Elgin Community College. Missy and I were walking down the stairs when he caught my eye. He smiled. I don't remember exactly what he said, perhaps because his attention toward me took me aback a little. Maybe it was just "hi."

Missy saw the look on my face and slowly shook her head. After he passed, she said, "His name is Jim, and, by the way, it would never work." She told me that he was the quiet, conservative type, and she reminded me that I was not. She thought I would get bored and that he would not know how to handle me. The funny thing was that I couldn't get him out of my head the rest of the day. Something about him seemed familiar.

Three months later, having finally received the go-ahead from my doctors, I prepared to start school again and drove to the College of DuPage to register. It was unbelievably warm for the Chicago area in

January (somewhere in the mid 20s), and I had the car window open and the radio playing. As I drove, I couldn't shake the feeling that I was heading in the wrong direction. I was almost to DuPage, but I just knew I was supposed to enroll at Elgin Community College. Everything in me resisted this prompting. As spontaneous as I was, I couldn't see changing all my plans at the last minute. Yet the prompting got the best of me, and I soon found myself in the registrar's office at E.C.C. signing up for classes. I thought I had lost my mind.

I grew up in the area, so I knew a lot of people who were attending E.C.C. Eventually, the idea of attending this new college settled in. On the first day of classes, my friend Vivian told me about this guy I really needed to meet. She said he had a strong faith in God and that we would make a great pair. I wasn't really looking for a boyfriend at the time, but I agreed to an introduction if we were ever all in the same place at the same time. Leaving it at that and dismissing the possibility in the near future, I headed off to my art class.

I walked into the classroom, found an empty seat, and glanced around. There, across the room, I saw a familiar face—the guy I had briefly met on the stairs three months earlier. I knew I was going to marry him. I don't know how, but I knew. Maybe it was "love at first sight." Maybe it was God knocking me in the head. (I admit I can be stubborn at times and sometimes need a good slap upside the head.) Whatever it was, I had no doubt about it.

A few days later, I was in the student lounge, soliciting clients for my friend's resume business. Jim was sitting there. I crept up to him and began fumbling with my words, speaking too quickly and not making much sense.

"Calmate!" he abruptly interrupted, holding his hands up in mock defense.

I stood there with a confused look on my face.

"Calm down," he translated with a slight smile.

I felt like disappearing. He declined the resume service, and I walked away feeling humiliated. A few days later in art class, we were instructed to paint using various shades of green. Jim, who was sitting next to me, leaned over and whispered with some urgency, "Can I borrow some green? All I have is red, blue and yellow." I thought he was joking. This was a college art class, and I'm pretty sure students were supposed to know that blue and yellow paint make green. However, he just kept looking at me with his eyebrows raised and a smirk on his face.

"Just mix your blue and yellow," I said. (It was his turn to be embarrassed.)

That kind of broke the ice between us. I still didn't know Jim's last name, but that was okay—the year had just started and there was plenty of time. I did want to get involved at E.C.C., so I decided to ask a friend about joining the student senate. I was told to give a resume to the student senate president, Jim Clapper. I asked Jim from art class if he knew who Jim Clapper was, and he graciously offered to take my resume and give it to him. He returned to me an official invitation from the student senate to attend the next meeting for an interview.

When I got there, I glanced around at the tables and saw the leaders of the student body looking very serious. The president sat at the head of the group. I looked up from the nameplate engraved "Jim Clapper," and there he was—the same "Jim" from art class, sitting with a mischievous grin on his face. I was beginning to understand the way he operated. The interview went well, and as I left, closing the door behind me, I heard them laughing. It turned out they were interrogating him about his interest in me. He so deserved it!

A few weeks later, Vivian invited me to a video dance (remember, it was the 80s!). I wasn't sure I wanted to go, but knowing that some of my guy friends from high school would be there, I agreed. I hoped that Jim would show up. Unbeknownst to me, he had received a similar invitation from Vivian, and he did come. The best way to tell you what happened next would be to let you read a letter that Jim sent to me afterward:

February 28, 1986

You mentioned the video dance—I didn't know you were going to be there. I stopped at Spiess to talk to Viv after work, before the dance. She had been trying to set me up with some girls the previous week—all of whom I was not interested in. That night she

mentioned someone else, but wouldn't tell me the name. I think I
had just met you the week before and I guessed you—hopefully. She
wouldn't say yes but wouldn't say no, which gave it away. I almost
hit the floor—or the parking lot—but I had to keep my composure
until I was away from Viv. I was glad to see you there! That was
the best E.C.C. dance I've been to—the only one too, but that's
beside the point.

Jim and I never danced together that night, but afterward we ended up at McDonalds, talking until they closed. I went home and told my mom that I was sure Jim was the guy I was supposed to marry. After that night, we were pretty much inseparable. I remember thanking God again and again for bringing Jim into my life, but I was still uncertain what Jim thought about our destiny, as we hadn't said "I love you" to each other yet.

About a week after the dance, I had an asthma attack and ended up in the emergency room. I came home exhausted and looking rather ragged. I was definitely not in any condition to see anyone. Jim surprised me by coming over unannounced. My mom let him in, and he walked into my room and told me how beautiful I was. I thought he must be blind. I knew I could not let go of him.

One day I asked if I could look at his art portfolio. I opened it up, and there was a drawing of black and white penguins going through a rainbow. Each of the penguins picked up the various colors of the rainbow as they passed through. I got goosebumps, because I felt that his drawing represented us.

Not long after that, Jim and I found ourselves in his comfy, oversized papasan chair. I was quietly contemplative, and he asked me what I was thinking. All that was running through my mind at the time were the words "I love you." I didn't share it at that moment, but when he asked me again, I used sign language to spell out "I love you." He then signed it back to me and said it out loud. We kissed, then, for the first time.

Later, Jim made the following entry into his journal:

April 28, 1986

Coll and I are going to pray together tomorrow night about us—it's going to be cool. She's everything I've prayed for—a Christian who enjoys having fun and doing crazy things and asks to get together and pray about us!

Seriously considering and asking the Lord if this is who He wants me to marry. It's strange, because even without asking I knew **** [name withheld] wasn't the one—I was scared at the thought of making that my last relationship . . .

Now I know Colleen's thought about it, and it's fairly certain it is to be—I'm not scared. It's weird, because thinking of marrying Colleen's not scary and I think I could make this my last relationship. It'd be great to be 19 & 18 and know that we've found each other and the Lord's given His blessings. Even waiting until '91 seems possible (maybe) as long as we know.

From the beginning, our relationship was based on Christ. We drove each other closer to God. I remember driving to Northern Illinois University with my friend Jennie. I told her that I believed Jim was the one and mentioned how cool it would be to see a rainbow. As soon as I said it, there was a rainbow in the sky. In fact, we actually drove under it. This was one of many confirmations for me of God's presence and active involvement in my life.

I soon learned that Jim was spending the summer in Spain and then transferring to Palmer Chiropractic College in Davenport, Iowa. I was also making plans to further my education. I always knew I wanted to major in either art or psychology, and I also knew that I wanted to work with people with special needs. By that summer, I decided to triple major. I did some research and discovered that the only college offering what I wanted was Augustana College in Rock Island, Illinois. I was pretty upset that this was my only option, because I knew Jim would be in Iowa. The thought of being in a long-distance relationship didn't excite me.

It was with mixed emotions that I received my acceptance letter from Augustana later that summer. Jim had left for Spain in May, two months earlier, and we were proving that we could manage without each other for a summer. But what about the long term?

I mentioned my concern to my friend Jill, who attended Augustana. She asked where Jim was transferring after Elgin Community College, and I said that he was going to Davenport, Iowa, to attend a school called Palmer.

"Palmer College of Chiropractic?" she said. I was surprised that she had even heard of it. She proceeded to inform me that Palmer College was five minutes from Augustana—the schools were on opposite banks of the Mississippi River (I never claimed to be good with geography). I called Jim in Spain right away. The little things kept adding up. God was giving me little nudges, guiding me toward what He wanted for my life.

Jim wrote me letters from Spain almost every day. Here is one of them:

> It seems like such a long time since we said goodbye in the airport— even now I look at your picture and wonder . . . how is it that a girl so precious could be waiting for me thousands of miles away? It's as if these pictures are of some "dream girl"—someone whom I hope to meet someday. But I have met you, and know you—perhaps as well as I know anyone. We are close because the Lord brought us together. He took my prayer and made it a reality!!! Colleen, I love you!

Our love continued to grow and mature in God. I had come a long way from the hurting and lonely person I had once been. God used my relationship with Jim to help me know that He answers prayers.

He used Jim to help me grow in other areas as well. We are so different, and iron does sharpen iron—although not without a few sparks! At Augustana, a couple of my psychology professors had Jim and I take a personality test. Jim scored all the way at one side of the range, and I scored all the way at the other. My professors shared their concern that our pending marriage wouldn't last because we were so different.

Jim listens mainly to AM talk radio while I have been known to blast rock music. Our first argument was about hunting. Jim loves to hunt, and I could never shoot "Bambi." The list goes on and on. Yet despite all of our differences, we always find that we enjoy being together and we refine and complement each other. More importantly, we come back to the fact that God put us together.

On Easter Sunday, Jim asked me to sit on his lap so we could pray together. Then he asked me if I would be his wife. He opened a heart-shaped box and showed me a ring he had designed himself. The stone was a heart-shaped diamond. He worked hard to pay for it, delivering pizzas and working the midnight shift at Roadway Express. I never expected anything fancy—I just wanted him—but I had never seen a more beautiful or more perfect ring. Of course, I said yes. Later that day as I was driving back to college with some friends, we all spotted another rainbow in the sky. I was amazed.

God uses people to make differences in our lives (and vice versa) to teach us timely lessons. Their part may be brief, like Alma's, but the impact of knowing them can be life-changing. God brought Jim into my life to help me understand my relationship with Him in the flesh.

Jim and I aren't perfect by any means. We've had moments in our marriage where we did not like each other and we wondered if we would really make it. Yet through it all, God has sustained us, and our love continues to deepen.

> Therefore what God has joined together, let man not separate.
>
> —Matthew 19:6

Chapter 3

Elizabeth, God's Gracious Gift

> We continually give thanks to God the Father of our Lord Jesus Christ (the Messiah), as we are praying for you, For we have heard of your faith in Christ Jesus [the leaning of your entire human personality on Him in absolute trust and confidence in His power, wisdom, and goodness] and of the love which you [have and show] for all the saints (God's consecrated ones), Because of the hope [of experiencing what is] laid up (reserved and waiting) for you in heaven. Of this [hope] you heard in the past in the message of the truth of the Gospel.
>
> —Colossians 1:3–5, AMP

I sat crying on the bathroom floor in the hospital. I was so thankful that it was made for only one and that I could lock the door and have some privacy. I don't particularly like public bathrooms, but this was the only refuge I could find at that moment. Everything seemed surreal, nightmarish. I kept thinking I would wake up. My body felt limp, and I could not stop the tears from running down my face. How could this be happening?

It was less than a year ago that I had been feeling the complete opposite. Things could not have been better. Here's an entry that Jim wrote in our baby's journal at the time:

The date is July 5, 1990, and it's about time we welcome you, in writing, and let you know how excited we are about your upcoming birth in November. We're here in Davenport, IA. We will have come a long way when you're old enough to read this. It will be interesting to see what God has planned for us.

I wrote:

We bought this book so that we can show you how much we love you already. The first time we heard your heartbeat was fantastic. Even before that, when we found out you were in my womb, we went crazy! So did everyone else. Your grandparents are going to spoil you rotten; they already are buying and making you things. They love you so much! Just a couple of weeks ago we saw you [by ultra-sound]. There are no words to explain how we felt. You were so active. The doctors tried to take a picture of your umbilical cord and you kicked it. In one picture it looks like you are smiling.

I love having you inside of me. I actually push a little to make you move so I can feel you. We just started reading Bible stories to you. We have a Christian lullaby tape that we play for you too. We love you so much and can't wait until you're on the outside!

P.S. You have a wonderful dad—you will know this already when you read this.

We had been married just eight months when I got pregnant. We were both still in school at the time. Jim was studying chiropractic, and I was getting my degrees at Augustana College. He was 23, and I was 22.

One day, out of the blue, my doctor told me that my oxygen levels were low. To make matters worse, we had an inferior insurance policy, so we had to depend on public aid—which meant we had to drive all the way to the hospital at the University of Iowa for treatment. It was an hour away.

We still enjoyed telling everyone we were having a baby. When I called one of my brothers, he left me on the phone after I told him and ran down the dormitory halls, telling everyone he was going to be an uncle. My father, who had wanted me to be a nun, threatened to punch

Jim (jokingly, of course!). Our moms began making plans and buying toys and clothes. Everyone was so excited.

I loved every minute of being pregnant. I had all the normal worries. I read at least 12 books to make sure I was doing everything right. I was an obsessed first-time mom. I ate well and got plenty of exercise.

Jim would be graduating one month prior to the delivery date, and he had already received a good job offer in Hawaii. I had been accepted to the University of Hawaii and was going to get my master's degree in special education. I planned to train dolphins on the side. However, the doctor Jim was going to work for in Hawaii was convicted of insurance fraud. It was really confusing, because we thought and hoped that Hawaii was where God wanted us to go. It seemed that everything we were planning—other than the baby—kept falling through. We got down on our knees and prayed for a healthy baby and for guidance so that we would know where to go once Jim graduated. We wanted God's perfect plan.

The months passed, and the closer we got to the due date, the more anxious we became. However, other things began looking up. Jim was offered a job with his mentor from back home. He had worked off and on there since undergraduate school. Jim's parents were nearby and still owned the house they lived in when he was born, so we could rent it from them. My family and friends gave me a shower, which provided everything I needed for when our baby came home. God was supplying all of our needs.

Only once, at the end of the pregnancy, did I have a hint that there was a problem. The doctor noticed that the baby hadn't grown in seven weeks. My heart dropped and I began to get nervous, but Jim said, "We just need to trust in God." God calmed my fears, and the hospital began various tests. All I could do was pray that there would be nothing wrong.

I told my friend Kerri that I could handle having a child with disabilities, but that it would be hard if he or she was born with heart and lung complications like me because I would know how hard it was when he or she struggled to breathe. I recall shrugging off a chill that went up my spine as I said those words. In hindsight, I think it was mother's intuition. Finally, the test results were back and a nurse came out to give us the news. The tests showed that everything was fine other than the baby being in the lower percentile for size. We were so happy that we dismissed the nurse's hesitation and the look in her eye. To this day, I believe she knew something else—that everything was not really going to be "fine."

During one of our many trips for routine pre-natal care, Jim came up with the idea that it would be great if a police officer stopped us for speeding when the actual time came for the baby to be born. That way, he would at least for once have an excuse for speeding.

When my labor began, Jim and I got in the car and sped toward Iowa City. Not far into the one-hour trip, Jim got his wish, and we were pulled over. Jim was anxious to tell the officer his story, but the cop was unimpressed, despite my groaning through clenched teeth as the contractions came on stronger. He didn't give us a ticket, thankfully, but he also didn't escort us the rest of the way. Much to our dismay, he actually followed us for several miles to make sure we went the speed limit.

Once we were safely at the hospital, things went as expected, and I was observed by no less than seven medical interns. I had intended on having a drug-free birth, but eventually I did ask for an epidural because the strain was affecting my asthma. It definitely took the edge off, but in just a couple of minutes my legs went completely numb. I couldn't feel them or move them at all. Ten minutes later when it came time to push, I felt disconnected from the lower half of my body. What a strange sensation!

As I contemplated this, the doctor told Jim to grab one leg and told an intern to grab the other. All modesty went out the window. I must say that Jim did well, but the intern, in his excitement, kept forgetting about my leg. He let go of it several times, and each time my leg just dropped like a rock. The intern would then apologize and support it again. I had some nasty bruises, but at that point I didn't care. I just wanted to meet my baby.

Elizabeth Christine Clapper was born at 1:00 P.M. on Monday, November 19, 1990. Elizabeth means "gracious gift from God," and that is exactly what she was. Her cry was soft and sweet. The nurse pulled a hand-knit stocking cap down over her ears and wrapped her tight in blankets. The hospital was so busy that I was able to hold her for two hours before they were able to perform the normal baby tests.

My mom and dad were at the hospital and came in to meet their granddaughter. My mom cradled the fifth generation of a first-born female baby in her arms. I remember saying to my dad, "Everything is going to be good." Yet even as I said these words, I gazed down at Elizabeth and tried to shake the feeling that somehow her soft cry was not quite right. *It's just new mom nerves*, I told myself.

Jim and I reluctantly gave Elizabeth up when the staff came in to take her to be tested. I started to get anxious when the tests took a little longer than they had expected. Eventually, a doctor came in to talk with us. He had tears in his eyes as he told us that Elizabeth had a double heart murmur and other characteristics that pointed to some serious congenital abnormalities. He said they would keep her for more tests. He reminded us to be thankful for the extended time we had just had with her and to pray that she would live through the night. We were, and we did.

When I was able to visit Elizabeth, I walked past a room where the parents were smoking and holding their newborn. Then I passed the nursery and saw all the healthy babies. People were looking in, their noses pressed to the big window, with smiles on their faces. I was about to enter a much different place—the Pediatric Intensive Care Unit (PICU), with its beeping monitors and hushed conversations. It is a place shrouded with concern and uncertainty. I kept thinking that Jim and I were supposed to be like the people down the hall who were smiling at their babies through the glass window. No—Elizabeth should be in my arms.

Instead, I was listening to specialists explain the different disabilities they had diagnosed our daughter with so far. They were drawing pictures of her heart to explain things like Tetralogy of Fallot and absent pulmonary valve. My mind was in a fog. Thirteen hours of labor and this emotional roller coaster ride was taking its toll. Amazingly, I was able to answer the specialists and ask many questions of my own. Again and again, they told us that our daughter may not make it through the night and that we needed to prepare ourselves. I understood what they were saying, but it seemed so surreal.

I had grown up working with children who were severely disabled. Along the way some of those children had died, so I was also familiar with death. I, too, had faced death on multiple occasions due to my congenital heart and lung complications. However, what I was experiencing now, with Elizabeth, went well beyond any trial I had ever gone through. I entered the PICU and walked over to see my daughter covered with monitors and wires. She had an IV in her head, and the sound of buzzing machines filled the air. Little did I know that this was just the first of many sleepless nights.

I saw many other things in the PICU. I saw a precious baby weighing one pound who was struggling for life. I saw her father, with dark circles under his eyes, looking like a fragile skeleton who might snap if someone touched him. I held David, a baby boy diagnosed as "brain dead," as his mother tried to convince herself that his involuntary movements meant he was trying to communicate. I accidentally walked into the PICU as the doctors were doing an emergency open-heart surgery on a young boy. I later hugged the boy's mom as she prepared to leave the hospital to plan his funeral. I saw children who had been beaten so severely that their once healthy little bodies now struggled to survive. Many children died in the units. Some had their parents with them; others died alone or in the arms of a loving nurse.

We stayed at the Ronald McDonald House during the first few days of Elizabeth's hospital stay. While we were there, we met many children who had cancer. On the first night, many of them, bald from the chemotherapy and wearing masks to protect them from germs, came up and greeted us. They were so mature, and in their eyes I saw a depth that many adults do not even possess. I heard parents crying as they received bad news. I could not think of anything worse than losing a child.

I saw miracles as well. I saw children in remission go home in the arms of their relieved parents. I saw a boy walk again, even though doctors and nurses thought he might be a "vegetable." I met a little girl whose brain tumor had disappeared. We prayed long and hard for that kind of miracle to happen to Elizabeth.

Believe it or not, we also had some fun times in the PICU. We had to wear masks to protect Elizabeth from germs, and after a long day of wearing masks and breathing in carbon dioxide, we got a little loopy! Once I put on the Jackson 5 song "ABC" for Elizabeth. A nurse was in the room at the time, and before the song was over, the nurse, Jim and I were all dancing in Elizabeth's room. Sometimes you just have to dance.

I was reading a book at the time about a pastor who had been thrown into a communist prison. He said that when prisoners lost their ability to laugh, their emotions were dead. I was determined there would be laughter and that Elizabeth would hear the joy that could be found in life. So we played music for her, constantly winding up the toy music box that played "Somewhere over the Rainbow." I sang lullabies and read the Bible to her. I rubbed her little webbed neck and her elf-like ears; both telltale signs of her congenital complications.

She was so beautiful to us. Her eyes were big and alert as they followed movements or just stared back at us intently. We stayed by her side as much as we could. I couldn't help but remember that if she had not been born at the University of Iowa Hospital, she would have had to have been flown to a place with a pediatric heart specialist. We had ended up there because we had inadequate health insurance. God had it figured out all along.

As test results came back, we found out that Elizabeth had DiGeorge's Syndrome, a rare immune system disorder that involved various congenital complications and a rare combination of severe heart and lung malformations.

God had closed those doors to Hawaii and opened the right ones. He had answered our prayers even though we didn't understand the situation at the time. We needed to have family and friends around us. They were there to eat Thanksgiving dinner with us at the hospital cafeteria. They were there to encourage us and pray for us. They were there to help us move our stuff to our new home in Illinois. They unpacked most of the items, set up the nursery and prepared meals, hoping that we would be able to bring Elizabeth home.

The doctors did more tests. They were concerned about Elizabeth's size and decided to postpone surgery for one month, believing that it would be easier to work on her heart when it was a bit bigger. So, we were given the all clear to take Elizabeth to Illinois and were told to choose a hospital to work with there. Before we left, however, they told us of all the signs of congestive heart failure to watch for and made sure we understood her medication schedule. They said that if everything went well we could go home for three to four weeks, but if things didn't go well, she would need to be hospitalized immediately. They also told us that she might die at home. Her little life was still in the balance, and we felt the pressure.

It was a mixed blessing being in our new home. I loved having Elizabeth at home but, as you can imagine, I didn't sleep much. The University of Iowa made calls and identified three hospitals in Chicago and one in Texas that were interested in taking her case. However, judging from our initial consultations, these hospitals seemed more intrigued by the rareness of her condition than with her as a person.

Just a few weeks earlier, my dad had met a pediatric heart specialist who was genuinely interested in Elizabeth and in us as a family. We chose to put her care into the hands of the pediatric cardiology team the doctor was associated with at The Heart Institute at Christ Hospital in Oak Lawn, Illinois. God came through for us again, and the hospital became our second home for the next few months. The staff were like a second family to us. We were also welcomed into the home of Li and Dolly; friends of a friend. They lived a few miles from the hospital and extended hospitality to us in many ways. (Dolly spoiled us with her fantastic blueberry muffins.)

Just a week and a half after bringing Elizabeth home, the hospital called us to tell us that the previous day's test had showed something wrong. They needed Elizabeth to come in for observation right away. After the call, I sat on the stairs and cried. I composed myself, and before we left, Jim set the camera on auto and joined Elizabeth and me on the couch for a family photo. It turned out to be one of our favorites.

Elizabeth needed surgery sooner than expected. Due to her condition, it was very hard for the nurses and specialists to draw blood. However, it was absolutely critical that they do a blood test on her before performing her first open-heart surgery. They needed to rule out any infection. If she had one, they would have to postpone the procedure. Now, I know a thing or two about the difficulties of having blood drawn. My veins are very small, and it usually takes numerous painful attempts to draw from them. Elizabeth gave the nurses and specialists the same challenge with her veins, so they finally opted to do an arterial cut down, which is an extremely painful procedure. They could not give her painkillers or sedatives because of the risk of her coding.

This was especially difficult for me, and I needed family and friends. I needed God. My mom and my friend Janet were there. They began to pray right away, and I am so glad they did, because I know God heard them. I understood that the procedure had to be done, but the pain I felt in knowing what my little girl was about to endure was excruciating. I reluctantly allowed the hospital staff to take her into another room, but as I heard her cries, every inch of me wanted to run in and stop them. Why did she have to go through this? I was supposed to be cuddling her and comforting her, yet I could do neither.

My mind flashed to a scene of Mary and Jesus. I cannot fathom what Mary felt watching her son endure such unbelievable pain as He was nailed to the cross. She knew He had to go through it, but I imagine she felt just as I did. I envisioned her wrestling with this awful scene. Her situation was much worse, because she had to watch as people spat on her son, beat Him and then put Him to death. In my case, the doctors, the nurse and the specialist wanted to help Elizabeth.

My pain did not necessarily subside, but at one of the worst points of my life God gave me some insight into His mother's heart. He took me to another spiritual level that can only be fully experienced through pain. Mary had to make a sacrifice, and the Lord must have given her great strength. I know she would have taken His place if she could, and I am sure a part of her was dying with Him. I also believe she was carried to a place that only she would understand—a true suffering that allowed her insight into the throne room of God. This was a rare gift nobody would volunteer to receive.

I was able to hold Elizabeth afterward. Every little muscle in her body relaxed as I held her close. I felt her tender baby's breath on my neck and smelled her sweet baby smell.

As I sat in her hospital room, I began to question everything I had done during the pregnancy. Irrational as it was, I remember one woman telling me that corn chips can cause problems. I spent a lot of time at the medical library looking for reasons as to "why" this might happen. Some people told me that if I prayed hard enough, I could save my baby. Some told me that Elizabeth had been born disabled due to my sins and that if I confessed them, she would be okay.

I stayed as optimistic as I could. I made sure the isolation unit was a pleasant atmosphere for Elizabeth despite the 19 meds she was on and the fact that her little body was covered with tubes and wires. I could not care for her as I would at home, but I could still pray for her and read the Bible to her. One of the best spiritual times of my life was in that isolation unit with my daughter.

Elizabeth was placed on a respirator after her first surgery. With all the tubing and tape, I could only see her eyes. Because she could not cry due to the tubing, I had to look at the monitors to judge her reactions. If she was upset, her blood pressure and heart rate would increase, and I would calm her. Her excitement at hearing our voices or feeling our touch was also evident.

Elizabeth went on to endure multiple open-heart surgeries, blood transfusions and other medical procedures. This was my experience as a first-time mom, and I felt so honored that God would allow me to have this beautiful child.

One day while I was grocery shopping, I spotted a woman who had Down's syndrome. The woman walked the aisles singing old show tunes and smiling as much to herself as to passersby. A few smiled back, but other shoppers shook their heads in disgust or pity. The woman was quite content, happy and oblivious to the scorn and shame projected by her fellow shoppers. Having had the opportunity and pleasure of working with many people with Down's syndrome, I found that I've learned more from them than I have ever taught them. Although they possess an I.Q. below worldly standards, I believe they are more capable in many ways than the majority of us.

Some with Down's syndrome do not know limitations, so they may react spontaneously. Contrary to what some people think, they do have the same feelings "normal" people. They see a butterfly and appreciate its beauty. They see someone they love and give them a hug without wondering what others will think. They see the many blessings that surround them and appreciate the smallest accomplishments. They are not incomplete because of their I.Q. Instead, they live fuller lives, and they experience it deeper because they retain their childlike faith.

> And he said to me, My grace is sufficient for thee: for my strength is made perfect in weakness. Most gladly therefore will I rather glory in my infirmities, that the power of Christ may rest upon me. Therefore I take pleasure in infirmities, in reproaches, in necessities, in persecutions, in distresses for Christ's sake: for when I am weak, then am I strong.
> —2 Corinthians 12:9–10, KJV

This chapter is dedicated to my friends with disabilities and to parents who are blessed with the honor of raising children diagnosed with disabilities. I have really understood that our very weaknesses can become our strengths for God's kingdom.

Chapter 4

An Easter Story

I'll never forget that phone call. It came at 3:00 A.M. on April 1, 1991. I was startled out of a restless sleep and quickly fumbled for the receiver so that our hosts, Li and Dolly, wouldn't wake up. Immediately, I knew it was the phone call that no parent wants to receive.

Two weeks before that phone call, the doctors had told us that Elizabeth's body was weakening and that there were no more aggressive measures they could take. "We're sorry," they said, and they meant it. We cried together. Later, in Li and Dolly's guest room, Jim and I decided to call our friend's father for some advice. He had just lost his wife, and they had lost infant twins years before. He told us there was no real answer as to how to get through it, but that he would pray for us. We thanked him and hung up the phone, still looking for answers.

Jim opened up the Bible and began reading 2 Corinthians 4 and 5. He paused, and we were silent for the next few moments as each of us let the truth of those words sink in. Then something unexpected and profound happened. Jim and I both felt, or rather experienced at the same time, the deepest, warmest and most overwhelming sense of peace. It not only covered us but also became part of us, or we of it—I'm not sure which. It was not just a feeling; it was as if we weren't in the room anymore and were being given a glimpse of heaven. That's exactly what I believe it was, and I know it could only have come from God. It was just like Paul wrote in Philippians about the peace that surpasses understanding that would guard our hearts and minds.

It was because of this moment, this gift, that we could honestly know that if this was what was in store for our daughter, and even more, we could release her into His care. As new parents, however, the two following weeks were still difficult. Elizabeth coded many times, and her body began to deteriorate. At one point, the nurse needed to stop the medication that kept her immobile so she could check her status. It had been a few weeks since she had last been allowed to move voluntarily, and the nurse warned me not to expect too much. She warned me that Elizabeth might not respond to me.

Instead, my daughter grabbed my finger and looked straight at me. The nurse and I both cried. We knew this was nothing less than a miracle. I saw Jesus in her eyes and a maturity that a baby does not usually possess. God gave me this moment with my daughter, and it is imprinted on my heart forever.

On April 1, I brought the phone to my ear. I knew in my heart that I was about to hear news that would devastate me, but I didn't want to believe it. The nurse could not legally tell me over the phone if Elizabeth had passed away, but she comforted me by saying that she was singing a lullaby to her. I shook as we drove to the hospital and remember anticipating my possible reaction when I saw her. There was no way of predicting what my response would be. She had been close to death for two weeks, but I knew this time would be different.

When we got to the hospital, I was relieved to find out that Elizabeth was still alive. My one prayer had been that if she were to die, I would be there to hold her. I had only been able to hold her three times during the past four months because of the machines she was hooked up to. The song that was playing in the background as we entered the ICU was "Can't Take My Eyes Off You" by Frankie Valli. My mom used to sing that song to me as a baby, and I, in turn, had sung it to Elizabeth many times.

It soon became obvious that despite the heroic efforts of the doctors and nurses, Elizabeth wasn't going to make it. It was just a matter of time. Time is a funny thing. Sometimes it races by so fast that you wonder where it has gone. Time is supposed to heal all wounds, but when you are waiting for your baby to go to heaven, the pain can be so overwhelming that your only defense is numbness.

I found it hard to even talk to her. The words stuck in my throat. All I could manage was to tell her how much I loved her over and over again. We read to her and played her favorite lullabies. While she was in isolation we had to wear masks, but now I was able to take off the mask and actually kiss her little face and feel her soft skin against my trembling lips.

Her condition worsened. I didn't want to see her suffering any more, but as a mother, I wanted desperately for her life to be spared. I was helpless. I could only pray to God for a stronger measure of that peace that He alone can give.

Our parents made it to the hospital. The doctors and nurses who had become second family to us surrounded us as I rocked Elizabeth in a chair. Jim stood right behind me and read the Bible to her. The doctor and nurse slowly took out the breathing tube and IVs as I cradled her. This was the first time in four months that I had held her with no wires or tubes. I saw her little tongue moving—an image that to this day both calms and haunts me.

The moments ticked by, and death hung in the air. The monitor flat-lined, the tone went steady, and Elizabeth slowly slipped away. The pain I felt was so intense, and yet there was a peace, too. I knew that she was going to see His face. I knew that for her there would be no more tears and no more pain, and for that I was relieved. She was going to be cradled in the same loving arms of My Father, who also held me during this time.

And just like that, her spirit was gone. Elizabeth had been promoted to heaven. It's hard to explain, but I actually felt the difference in her body. After a while, we handed her to the nurse who took her, bathed her and wrapped her in a white blanket. I laid her down on the bed for the last time. That is my last image of her. We chose not to see her in a casket but to remember her swaddled tightly in a warm blanket.

My Aunt Peg saw a rainbow that day. It confirmed to us, once again, that Elizabeth went home.

I can't imagine what our parents were going through as they watched. It was the day of my parent's twenty-fourth wedding anniversary, but there would be no celebration this year. Both sets of grandparents grieved not only the loss of their granddaughter but also the loss of our innocence. They carried a burden for us, and I know it was so difficult for them to go through this with us. Yet their prayers sustained us.

We left the hospital without our daughter and made the long drive home. It was a sunny day, and even though I felt the full range of emotions, an undercurrent of peace was always within reach. As I entered our house, it seemed almost foreign to me. I had lived at the hospital or at a friend's house for four months.

I was numb, but I knew I had to begin the task of planning Elizabeth's funeral. Even with the warmth of the sun coming through the nursery window, I felt cold and lonely. My arms already ached to hold Elizabeth just one more time—a feeling that I would come to recognize as a constant companion.

Jim saw to the arrangements for the headstone while I took care of the rest of the arrangements, including the process of choosing a casket—which turned out to be white. It was so small and reminded me that it had only been a few months since I had chosen a crib for Elizabeth.

We decided to have a private burial and then hold a memorial service to celebrate her life. That day is somewhat of a blur; it was a Thursday. I remember trying to put on make-up and thinking it was so frivolous. I recall stepping into the car, knowing that I was on my way to bury our baby. She was the first to be buried in that particular cemetery. As we pulled up, I saw the casket and a hole in the ground.

My friends Kris and Angie handed me pink roses to put on Elizabeth's casket. It was so strange to be placing the same kind of flowers I had received for her birth on her casket. The pastor spoke about Easter, which seemed appropriate.

The memorial service was next, and the church was packed. We sang songs, and Jim and I stood up and testified about God's faithfulness and about how Elizabeth had changed our lives. As I sat back down, one of my brothers grabbed my other brother's hand, and they began to cry. That's when I lost it. I was the big sister who had always felt the need to protect them, and this time I couldn't. I could not take away their pain or their tears. I knew they cried for their loss and ours. I knew that some of those tears were for me. I felt helpless and yet so blessed to have such love from my brothers.

Shortly after, my husband, Jim, wrote the following words in Elizabeth's journal:

It has been one week since God welcomed our daughter into His kingdom of eternal peace and comfort. We will miss her, our little angel. We do, however, have the knowledge that she'll be waiting for us when we leave this earth and also enter the glory of heaven.

Elizabeth Christine Clapper died on April 1, 1991, at 6:50 A.M., of respiratory failure. She fought for every one of the 133 days she had, and she taught us much about courage and determination. She also forced many of us to our knees. The morning of April 1, a nurse named Ellen called us at 3:00 A.M. to tell us that Elizabeth was not doing well. By the time Colleen and I arrived at PICU, five minutes later, Elizabeth had flat-lined and been brought back. I believe this, her second glimpse at the future, was enough to convince her that her purpose had been fulfilled on earth and that it was time to go home. She was kept "alive" with very large doses of epinephrine, an adrenalin-like drug.

When Colleen and I heard this, we asked that they not continue the injections. Colleen was very sympathetic, having had adrenalin shots for asthma as a child. She knew the side effects included heart and chest pain, dizziness and nausea, and in such large doses as Elizabeth was receiving, the discomfort she would experience just to keep her heart beating temporarily was unwarranted. After discussing this with the surgeon, the very gifted and blessed Dr. Ilbawi, he agreed that aggressive measures were no longer beneficial. But not wanting to give up totally, he started an IV drip of epinephrine to last until 11:00 that morning, after which she would receive no more.

Elizabeth's blood pressure had been dropping into the low forties, at which time they would administer the drug. The last injection was at approximately 5:45 P.M., which increased her blood pressure, and then the IV was supposed to sustain her at that level. But Elizabeth had had enough—enough of the ventilator tubes, the many, many medications and the surgeries. Her body was growing weaker, but her spirit was strong! Our little angel was a fighter and we loved her—we still do. As 2 Corinthians 4:16 says, her earthly body was wasting away but her spirit was being renewed daily—by the prayers of the saints, especially Elizabeth's mom. Colleen was at her side every day reading scriptures, praying, singing and playing Christian tapes. Elizabeth knew she was loved and appreciated as a gift from God. Her spirit was strong!

At 6:45 A.M. her little body couldn't take anymore, and her purpose here on earth was met. It all seems like a dream now. She was here and now she is gone. She was set free at 6:50 A.M. The monitors displayed a flat-line, her little tongue stopped moving, and her chest stopped pulsating. Her Christian lullaby still played, and I laid down the children's Bible I had just finished reading from and we cried. I imagined her looking down on the whole scene and saying, "Thank you for everything. I love you, too. I'm all right now and I'll be waiting!" Then she was escorted to the gates of heaven.

We said goodbye to one who briefly made an appearance in this world, taught us many things, and then went home. Now we must continue with the lessons learned. Our purpose is to journey through this life, working unto the Lord, praying without ceasing, rejoicing always, giving thanks and, most importantly, spreading the gospel.

A few weeks after Elizabeth died, I went to the gravesite and just broke down. The pain was so intense, like none I had felt before. I asked God if He understood how I felt. Did He know how bad my arms ached to hold her? In the gentlest way, I felt Him say, "Yes, I watched my Son die." I understood Easter before Elizabeth died, but I gained a deeper understanding of it after she died. Death is inevitable. So is eternity. It just comes down to where we are going to spend it. Everything I have learned and experienced points to a Savior, a God who loves us fully and unconditionally. A God who gives us hope to continue on.

> We are hard pressed on every side, but not crushed; perplexed, but not in despair; persecuted, but not abandoned; struck down, but not destroyed. We always carry around in our body the death of Jesus, so that the life of Jesus may also be revealed in our body. For we who are alive are always being given over to death for Jesus' sake, so that his life may be revealed in our mortal body. So then, death is at work in us, but life is at work in you.
>
> —2 Corinthians 4:8–12

Chapter 5

Redemption

About a month after the funeral, I was driving back from a bridal shower when I heard a song on the radio that touched me so deeply I had to pull over and have a good cry. I was still in mourning for my daughter, and I wanted to know what she was doing in heaven. I looked out the window and there it was—a double rainbow. I could picture Elizabeth and my grandfather, who had passed away within a month of her, giggling together.

The next few weeks were tough. Oddly, I could still smell the antiseptic from the hospital, even though I wasn't there. I would wake up in my bedroom and forget that I was home. I took walks when I could, and those seemed to help. I attempted to answer all the phone messages and letters I had received and found solace in that—just knowing so many people cared enough to contact Jim and me meant a lot. They even set up fund-raisers to help us cover our bills.

One of the fund-raisers was a comedy night sponsored by the Phi Rho Sorority at my alma mater, Augustana College. Some of my sorority sisters asked if we thought it was okay to do a comedy night in light of the seriousness of the situation. I thought it was perfect! I was touched by all the teachers and professors who attended and was glad it was a night full of laughter. Many people feel they should bury themselves in their misery after a tragedy. They feel laughter cheapens the memory of the person they have lost. But it doesn't, and it's necessary for survival. So I laughed when I could and cried when I had to.

There were dedications and memorials. Someone even wrote a song in memory of Elizabeth. We were in awe of the support we received. I was most affected by those who wrote to tell us that their lives had changed through our daughter's experience. Many of them now realized how short life is. They wanted to learn more about the gift of eternal life that Jesus promises.

Despite the circumstances, my relationship with Jim grew even stronger. Statistics show that 80 percent of couples who lose a child end up in divorce. We made the decision to allow each other to grieve in our own personal way. We didn't place expectations on each other's grief. We knew that even though our faith was being tried, we had to keep praying together. And we allowed ourselves to laugh together, too.

One evening, we decided to have a picnic on our living room floor. I am embarrassed to say that we listened to Dr. Demento—a comedian who is into strange songs—on the radio. After we were done eating, we took two spoons and dove into a quart of Hagan Daaz ice cream. We talked about losing Elizabeth and the fact that we were $900,000 dollars in debt due to the medical bills. We didn't know if we could have children again, and we were completely unsure about the future. But we still had each other and, more importantly, God. As we laughed about the dumb songs, we realized that all we really could do was surrender. We had to give it all over to God and trust that He was in control. That moment is one of my favorite memories.

I needed to get my mind focused on something, and health insurance seemed like a good place to start. It's always been difficult for me to get insurance due to my congenital heart and lung complications. I decided to enroll in graduate school, as I knew I had a better chance of getting insurance if I were a student. I began to pursue my master's degree in art therapy. I sent in the appropriate forms and applied for a scholarship. We didn't have any money, so, in a way, this all seemed as impossible as it was impractical. I wanted to start as soon as possible, but without the scholarship, I wouldn't be able to attend summer classes. I was promptly informed that I had been placed on a long list of students who also wanted a scholarship. Still, I felt God was leading me to do this, and I believed I was supposed to trust Him.

On a Friday night, Jim, my brother Larry and I were watching a movie and eating pizza at our house. Graduate classes were scheduled to start the following Monday, and I was already resigned to the fact that I would not be attending them. My master's degree was not to be—at least, that is the thought that ran through my mind. I should have remembered that God enjoys doing things at the last minute and in unexpected ways.

Suddenly, the phone rang. It was the administrator of the program, calling to inform me that he would see me in class on Monday. I started to protest, reminding him about my finances. He interrupted me with the news about which he had really called: I was being awarded the scholarship. I was speechless. He just laughed and said, "See you in class on Monday!"

The following week we received another call—this time from the Illinois Department of Public Aid. The lady who had been working on our medical case asked if I was sitting down. I was just about to place myself on the couch when she told me that all of Elizabeth's medical expenses were going to be covered. She had just found a provision that qualified us for this blessing. God had come through for us again.

I still had one more request for God. I always believed that I would have children, but the doctors had been telling me from the beginning that my body might not be able to carry a baby. Now, having lost Elizabeth, I wondered if they might be right. It was so difficult for me to think that I would not be able to get pregnant again, especially after carrying a child and then losing her. Despite the difficulties during the pregnancy, I had loved the whole experience.

I desperately wanted to feel a child inside me again. Many of my family members and friends were getting pregnant. I wasn't envious, but it was awkward at times. It was hard for some of them to even tell me they were pregnant. I would go to baby showers and once in a while, right in the middle of the joyous event, the expecting mother would glance over at me with sad eyes. I was thankful for their concern, but I didn't want them to feel bad or uncomfortable.

I also wanted to give Jim another child, and I often felt guilty for not being able to do so. He never blamed me. In fact, he was completely supportive during the whole experience. We both wanted a family. If we couldn't have another child naturally, then we would adopt. As I was praying about all of this, a rainbow appeared in the sky. I sensed it was God's promise to me that one way or another, we would have another child.

The day before my twenty-fourth birthday, I went into the hospital for a catheterization. The doctors wanted to see if the oxygen levels in my body were high enough to carry a baby. These doctors had been Elizabeth's cardiologists and were like family to me. I had once even gone out with them to eat BBQ ribs. (I must caution anyone who is invited to eat ribs with surgeons that the dinner conversation can be quite bizarre. Really, though, we had a great time!)

As for the catheterization, I was a little uncomfortable with the procedure because I had become so close to the physicians and nurses. They gave me some Valium, though, and soon I was in la-la land. The doctors had a little fun with me by asking me questions, knowing that I would slur my answers. It was actually quite humorous, and it helped to alleviate some of the anxiety I was feeling about the situation and the pending results of the test.

The procedure went well and I was brought to a hospital room on the same floor where Elizabeth had been. Even though I was an adult, I was seen as a pediatric cardiology case because my condition was congenital. I was supposed to rest there for a few hours to ensure that my blood clotted correctly. So, as I did, I thought of how strange the whole situation was. I was lying down the hall from where my daughter had spent three-fourths of her short life and had died five months earlier. I prayed that whatever the results of the test were, I would be able to accept God's will for the situation.

When they gave me permission, I walked to the PICU to say hi to the nurses whom I had grown to care for so much during our daughter's experience. I was doing okay emotionally, but I felt very weak physically. When I got to the PICU, I collapsed to the floor. My blood had not clotted completely, and they escorted me back to my room. The doctor decided that I needed to stay overnight. I could not imagine staying the night in the some hospital where my daughter had died. I cried at first, but by God's grace, I was able to make it through the night.

Dr. Husayni came in the next morning with a little smirk on his face. He put his back to the wall and slid down to sit on the floor. Dr. Husayni always had a twinkle in his eye, and I was ready for his news. I knew him well enough to know that what he was about to say would be positive. He told me the test showed that I could still have a baby. That was the best news Jim and I had heard in a long time. I conceived that week.

Jim and I began planning our lives again. I was a little nervous about our baby at times—who wouldn't be after what we had been through—but God also gave me a sense of confidence. I knew this baby was from Him and that I had to trust that this child's life was in His hands. I dealt with morning sickness, afternoon sickness and night sickness on a daily basis. That made it difficult to attend classes and work—I had three part-time jobs—but I managed.

Things were going fine until I started to bleed during the fourth month. Jim and I cried all the way to the ER. We also prayed. We kept asking God the famous question, "why?" My memories of that night are hazy. I think I shut down a little bit, but they ended up telling me my baby was going to be okay. I had to go on bed rest until the delivery, which meant that I had to discontinue working and put my master's degree on hold.

A few months later, on Valentine's Day, I went in for an ultrasound. Jim could not attend because he had to work. We agreed ahead of time that I would find out the sex of the baby and would tell him after work. We wanted to know if it was a boy or a girl, because we wanted to identify with him or her as soon as possible and for as long as we could. That night, I put out a bouquet of balloons and made a sign that said, "Happy Valentine's Day, Dad . . . Love, James Michael." Jim was extremely happy. I don't think I could have given him a better Valentine's Day surprise.

On May 22, 1992, I was doing my sister-in-law's hair for a high school event. As I was placing a curler in her hair, I had a major contraction. It was strong enough for me to accidentally flip the curler in the air. For the past three days I had experienced contractions, but I knew this was it. The time had come!

I called Jim, but I couldn't reach him right away. The contractions were getting stronger and coming more quickly. I tried to smile through them so as not to scare Sarah, but I don't think I succeeded. Sarah didn't have her driver's license yet and I was in no position to drive, so we were stuck. Finally, about 40 minutes later, we got in touch with Jim, and he picked me up and rushed me to the hospital. My mom was able to meet us there. She was gripping the curtain of the delivery room window as she watched me go through labor pains. I saw the joy on her face as her grandson entered the world. We had a healthy baby boy.

Jim and I left for home on a Sunday morning. We decided to stop by our church, as it was on the way. We knew the worship service was just about finished. As people poured out of the church, they stopped to look in the window of the car at our son. These were the same people who had been at our daughter's funeral. Now, they were crying tears of joy. God gives and He takes away, but He is always good.

A year later I got pregnant again. We didn't plan it, but we were still excited. I was ready for another baby. This pregnancy, however, would prove to be even more difficult than the last. Within a week of becoming pregnant, I started having heart palpitations. Due to the rarity of my condition, I was taken to the Mayo Clinic in Minnesota to have tests done. Their facility is phenomenal, and while I was there they were able to uncover new information concerning my medical conditions. They administered the new medications, and it looked like things were going to improve.

Still, I was disturbed by a meeting we had with the geneticist. She had done a thorough background on both of our families and had come to the conclusion that we should think of aborting our baby because he or she had a 50 percent chance of contracting my heart and lung complications or other congenital abnormalities. I felt sad for this woman. She had either never grasped the true concept of life or had let her medical training overshadow the preciousness of it. Sadder still is the number of babies that have been aborted at her suggestion.

There was absolutely no way we would abort this child. Every parent wants to hear that his or her baby is going to be perfectly healthy, and it is so easy to convince yourself that it wouldn't be "fair" to bring an unhealthy baby into the world. Jim and I had to draw on our faith in

God, our hope for the future, and our love for this baby. We chose life. Whatever the outcome, we would love and provide for our baby.

The following months seemed to go well. My weight gain, the growth of the baby and the baby's heartbeat were all normal. I was getting more and more excited. Then, one day, I felt a lump on my right breast. I wasn't quite sure what to make of it, so I called the doctor to set up an appointment. The doctor ordered tests right away.

My cousin, Rosemary, had died from breast cancer. We had been very close. She was one of those people you couldn't help but enjoy being around. Being with her just made you smile. She had been pregnant when doctors discovered that her breast cancer had returned. After Elizabeth died, she had sent cards almost every week for months. Her messages were so encouraging and were often about God's promise of heaven. When I heard that her cancer had spread, I made plans to go see her. I had been on bed rest with James, but I was given clearance to go.

I called Rosemary to tell her I was coming the next day, but she could barely speak. I told her over the phone that I loved her. The next day as I was getting ready to leave, I received a call saying that she had passed away. I gave the cards that she had given me to her husband to encourage him as they had encouraged me. Rosemary fought every step of the way, and thinking of her gave me strength as I went to have the tests performed.

The doctor confirmed that the lump in my breast was a tumor. When I heard the news, my main concern was for the baby. The doctor would have to do the biopsy while I was awake. I could not be sedated due to my pregnancy and my lung complications, so all I could have was a local anesthetic. Thankfully, Jim was allowed to be in the room with me. His medical background was comforting. He watched the surgery, and I saw his face as the doctor removed the tumor. He had a gentle smile, and I felt that it was going to turn out well.

The days following the biopsy were stressful. I had to make sure that I didn't allow fear to take over. Finally, the results came back. The tumor was benign. After the doctor called with the news, I reached down and felt my stomach. Just then, the baby decided to kick. I knew this little one had a profound calling. The adversity surrounding this pregnancy had been so thick. I felt like my baby was already overcoming such large odds that something special was in store for his or her life.

Joshua Caleb Clapper was born on March 21, 1994. He was handsome and healthy.

God saw Job as a righteous and upright man, but He allowed Satan to afflict Job in order to test him to see if he would stay faithful to God. Job lost his possessions and children. He experienced severe sores all over his body, and he faced other trials. Job said the following:

> "Oh, that my words were recorded, that they were written on a scroll, that they were inscribed with an iron tool on lead, or engraved in rock forever! I know that my Redeemer lives, and that in the end he will stand upon the earth. And after my skin has been destroyed, yet in my flesh I will see God; I myself will see him with my own eyes—I, and not another. How my heart yearns within me!"
> —Job 19:23–27

I do believe God is the Redeemer! I believe even unanswered prayers are answered. I may not always like the outcome, but I have learned (and am still learning) that God sees the overall picture. I pray to have such a faith like Job!

Chapter 6

Prison Ministry

Then the King will say to those on his right, "Come, you who are blessed by my Father; take your inheritance, the kingdom prepared for you since the creation of the world. For I was hungry and you gave me something to eat, I was thirsty and you gave me something to drink, I was a stranger and you invited me in, I needed clothes and you clothed me, I was sick and you looked after me, I was in prison and you came to visit me."

—Matthew 25:34–36

About a year after James was born, I went back to school and started attending graduate classes at Northern Illinois University. It was a 60-mile round trip that took me by a youth prison just outside of town. Every time I drove by, I felt a tug on my heart as I thought about those boys whose lives had gone wrong.

One day as I passed the prison, I heard the sound of two young men crying as clearly as if they were in the car with me. I shook my head, trying to shake the sound of cries away, hoping they would disappear. They didn't. All the way to class, I had the feeling that something horrible had happened. That night, I went to class and tried to focus on other things.

The next week as I drove past the prison again, I deliberately slowed down and listened. I'm not sure what I expected to hear—maybe a repeat of the eerie experience—but nothing unusual happened. I did, however, feel a deep concern for those boys, and the tugging on my heart was even stronger. I went to class expecting it would be like every other session. It wasn't. The professor started by announcing that the youth prison needed an art therapist and that the position would begin right away. A chill ran up my spine and I shivered. My professor told us that two young men had recently committed suicide there. It had been the same night I had heard the cries.

I was stunned.

I knew I was supposed to go, but it didn't make sense. Prison work didn't fit into my plans, which revolved around doing an internship with special needs children. It would also mean scrapping the rough draft of my thesis. I was comfortable with my plans. Working with people who have special needs had been my passion ever since I was a little girl, and I had been sure it was the direction I would pursue. But God had other plans.

To further complicate the situation, I was pregnant with Josh. I had to make a tough decision, because my first concern was for my unborn child. I knew without a doubt that the prison ministry was a calling from God. But how could I explain going to work in a prison while I was pregnant? It seemed almost irresponsible, and yet every time I thought or prayed about it, I felt peace. I knew God would protect me. I asked Jim to pray, and he knew also that this was God's plan. Even my father-in-law received confirmation in prayer. So I began applying my education in the prison system, and in return was educated in a whole new way.

The prison itself was a very dark place, but not because of the lack of physical light. There was just an awful, oppressive feeling. I was actually thankful to be pregnant at the time, because every kick the baby made reminded me of everything good and brought me a measure of hope in such an evil place.

One of my responsibilities was to apply art therapy to the inmates on suicide row. Suicide row was in a separate part of the prison where prisoners were sent if they were either a suicide risk or had actually attempted it. I was assigned to work with the toughest cases. I was totally unprepared for what I would find there.

I was also supposed to administer psychological evaluations to prisoners when they arrived at the facility. It was a screening process designed to assess, among other things, their sociability, levels of despondency or depression, and overall aggressive tendencies. This time was critical, because the first contact with prisoners was when impressions were made and trust was established.

I made it a point not to read any of the inmate's files prior to meeting and evaluating him. That way, I could remain unbiased and maintain my focus on him as a person. This would have been much more difficult if I had read about the inmates in advance. So I met them, evaluated them, and then read their files. Some of the crimes these prisoners committed were truly hideous. Many times, my stomach turned as I read about the things they had done and what their victims had endured.

I wouldn't for a second begin to condone what they had done, but I came to realize this lifestyle was all they had known. Some had been raised like animals, void of love and nurturing, with no instruction in right and wrong. Their hearts had turned to stone at an early age and their consciences never developed enough to influence their actions. How then could I even begin to minister to these young men? How could I possibly relate to their situations? Personally, I knew I couldn't. It could only be done through God's grace.

I will never forget one boy who fidgeted nervously and shook violently with fear. He looked like an injured animal unable to run from a predator. He was small, and I knew he understood that the worst was yet to come from the other inmates. He would take his turn being "initiated" and would find his place in the order of things. I won't go into details, but I saw his desperation, and my heart sank for him. He had come from the streets and had learned to survive there. Here, his challenge would be the same. It was another world ruled by evil and hatred.

The inmates approached everything and everyone with initial suspicion. They never gave trust lightly; it had to be earned. There was so much loneliness. Yet for all its darkness, for some this world was safer than being outside the barbed and razor wire. Many times the inmates, on hearing that they were going to be released, would try to ensure their continued incarceration. They would make escape attempts to get re-arrested or start fights with other inmates or guards. As a result, most had years added on to their sentences. They were grateful for it.

They had accepted the darkness of the prison and even found comfort in it. For them, it represented the lesser of two evils.

My mission in the prison was to introduce the inmates to another option. I needed to remain strong and draw strength from beyond myself. So I prayed and asked others to pray for me.

One morning, my prayer partner, Bonilee, called me with a warning. She told me the Lord had spoken to her and said I would be seeing 'black eyes' in the prison. That's all she could tell me. I had seen hateful glares, lustful looks and blank stares, and I knew better than to discount her advice. As it turned out, later that day I found out exactly what she had meant.

I was alone on the counselors van that shuttled us between the gate and the buildings when it abruptly stopped halfway between. My pulse quickened as I realized that an inmate van had broken down. I heard the pounding of my heart as I saw the prisoners being transferred to my van. The seats faced the center, not forward like normal vans, and an enormously muscular inmate with the "blackest" eyes I had ever seen sat down across from me. When I say "black eyes," I mean it in every sense—physically and spiritually. His stare was creature-like. Then he spoke, uttering a verbal threat toward me.

If the driver heard the inmate, he pretended not to. Either way, he made no attempt to intervene. There was a prisoner next to me, however, who covered his mouth with his hand and whispered to me, "Look him straight in the eyes, and do *not* let him know you're scared." I had instinctively crossed my hands over my stomach, and at that moment I felt Josh kick. I wanted to run off the bus, but that wasn't an option because it would have put me in even more danger. It was below zero outside, and there were more prisoners outside and no guards in sight.

So I did the only thing that came to mind: I prayed and stared straight ahead until my unfocused vision blurred his image into wavy colors. The van stopped with a jolt and the prisoners shuffled out—all of them, thankfully. Once I was alone again, I waited an extra few seconds and then made my way to the counseling office. I was unharmed, but definitely unnerved.

I did not want to return the next day. I was done with this "mission field" and was sure that my professor would understand. Bonilee called me again the next morning and told me that I needed to go back. She was confirming what I already knew. There was no escaping the call that God had placed on my heart. Being in that prison was like fighting on the frontlines of a battlefield, but I recognized God's protection and knew that He was holding me in His hands.

That day, I saw a man entering the prison ahead of me with a Bible in his hand. As we waited for the van, I nodded at his Bible and asked him what he was doing there.

"I'm here to bring these young men hope," he said.

He had no way of knowing about my experience the day before, but he went on to tell me that he believed I also had a special purpose there and that God wanted me to know that He was protecting my baby and me. Thank God that He confirms His intentions. I needed that encouragement, and it renewed my strength to continue the fight.

> For our struggle is not against flesh and blood, but against the rulers, against the authorities, against the powers of this dark world and against the spiritual forces of evil in the heavenly realms.
>
> —Ephesians 6:12

Inside the prison, much like anywhere else, people try to fill their emptiness with any number of things that ultimately prove to be disappointing and unsatisfying. To that end, the prison was full of inmates who were practicing satanic worship. To make matters worse, one of the counselors was sadistically influencing the prisoners' minds by giving them horror novels and other "dark" reading materials and manipulating them toward evil.

As an art therapist intern, I would have the inmates use art as a non-verbal means of communicating. I found this to be effective, given the fact that having them sit around "sharing their feelings" was not an option. When I saw the inmates' drawings, I could immediately see the results of the other therapist's influence. Their drawings were twisted and desperate, full of rage and hopelessness, and reflected their situation and state of being. God gave me compassion for these prisoners and the ability to see their worth through Jesus' eyes. I tried to be an example of His love for them. I realized that even though I hadn't committed the crimes they had, I was no more deserving of God's grace than they were. The experience I had with these young men gave me insight into God's heart. I could now envision Jesus sitting with tax collectors, prostitutes and thieves, and I could start to understand His love for them all.

I told these young men about Jesus and began to see changes in some of them. One man came to know Jesus in a profound and lifesaving way. I saw joy in his eyes for the first time as Jesus replaced his emptiness with the only thing that really satisfies: Himself. And he wasn't the only one. Another young man, who was always drawing horrible images when we first started his sessions, ended up drawing a cross. As some of the inmates became Christians, I saw them embrace hope.

I also began to earn the respect of some of the other inmates. They now saw me as someone they wanted to "protect" from other inmates and guards. When you first go into a prison, the prisoners are generally thought of as the bad guys. Most people would have associated them with the darkness I felt when I first entered that place, but as it turned out, some of the guards were even worse. They taunted me and ridiculed me. On more than one occasion, prisoners came to my aid and protected me.

I became like a big sister to many of the young men. Most of them were in gangs, and they explained their creeds, symbols, secret alphabets and tattoos to me. The gangs were the only family they knew. They even took bets for french-fries on whether I was having a boy or a girl. One young man was really excited about the baby. He was particularly excited at the thought that my child would have a different life than he had. During one of his counseling sessions, he recited the lyrics to a song he had memorized. It spoke about finding strength while discovering the hero inside of you. He told me that the lyrics were exactly what he wanted for himself. He asked if I thought he could ever be a hero, and when I answered yes, he broke down and cried. No one had ever encouraged him before. His entire life had been one hurtful experience after another. Every once in a while I hear that song on the radio, and inevitably my eyes well up with tears.

I pass that prison often and think about those young men and what happened to them. Sadly, some of their lives never changed, but I smile when I remember the lives that were changed forever. Since my time there, a sports complex has been built right next to the correctional facility. I wonder if the inmates watch through the fences and see parents cheer for their kids playing soccer or football. My heart breaks as I remember these young men who never had that kind of opportunity. I am also reminded of the many young people who will never hear words of love or encouragement and will end up in jail. Yet I know that even for these, there is a chance for redemption—a life filled with hope and purpose. While it won't change the circumstances of their imprisonment, it will change their hearts and eternal destiny.

Some of my favorite parts of the Bible are where Jesus would sit and eat with prostitutes, tax collectors and others considered outcasts. He never condoned sin or, as I discussed in this chapter, criminal activities. He convicted people but didn't condemn them. He would actually get frustrated with the hypocritical actions of "religious" people.

You may be a prisoner, a prostitute or someone with a culturally "taboo" illness. You might be in a physical, emotional or spiritual prison . . . you feel that you are alone and not worthy. Jesus came to earth just for you. His arms are open, and He can show you a freedom that you could never have imagined. Not only did He create you, but He also loves you.

> But the Scripture declares that the whole world is a prisoner of sin, so that what was promised, being given through faith in Jesus Christ, might be given to those who believe.
> —Galatians 3:22

> Jesus said to them, "I tell you the truth, the tax collectors and the prostitutes are entering the kingdom of God ahead of you. For John came to you to show you the way of righteousness, and you did not believe him, but the tax

collectors and the prostitutes did. And even after you saw this, you did not repent and believe him."

—Matthew 21:31–32

He [Jesus] went to Nazareth, where he had been brought up, and on the Sabbath day he went into the synagogue, as was his custom. And he stood up to read. The scroll of the prophet Isaiah was handed to him. Unrolling it, he found the place where it is written: "The Spirit of the Lord is on me, because he has anointed me to preach good news to the poor. He has sent me to proclaim freedom for the prisoners and recovery of sight for the blind, to release the oppressed, to proclaim the year of the Lord's favor."

—Luke 4:16–19

Chapter 7

Counseling Survivors of Satanic Ritual Abuse

My earliest recollection of the occult is from the eighth grade. I had a friend named Mike who seemed to be a normal 13-year-old boy, except that a large section of his hair was dyed blond. I never thought to question him about this, nor did I realize it was part of an occult ritual in which he participated.

One day, he was drawing an upside-down cross on a table in our art classroom. Since I'd been raised in a Christian home, this mocked everything I had been taught to believe. The cross he drew looked rather frightening, and I half jokingly reached across and tried to erase it. He grabbed my wrist and squeezed tightly. There was a message in his grasp, but it was the look in his eyes that sent chills up and down my spine. His eyes did not even seem human, and I said a silent prayer. I continued to insist on erasing the upside-down cross despite his resistance. I later found out from a mutual friend (and later confirmed with Mike himself) that his family was involved in the occult.

My next exposure to the occult was a few years later through a high school teacher who was mentoring me. She was the same one who introduced me to existentialism. It seemed innocent enough at first—at least until she began encouraging me to engage in the metaphysical by attempting to move objects using only my mind. I knew then that this was crossing a line I did not want to cross. I also learned about other gateway activities to the occult that straddled that line, including Ouija boards, tarot cards, horoscopes and psychic readings.

During my prison art therapy internship, I met an inmate named John who had been taught occult practices by a corrupt pastor. John had memorized whole books of the Bible, but he was taught to hate it. He discussed his religious beliefs with me and told me of his experiences, which included out-of-body experiences, or astral projections. John also believed that he saw demons and had been visited by beings who revealed themselves in spiritual forms. From biblical times to the twenty-first century, there have been many references to such occurrences. The apostle Paul, writing a letter to the Ephesians, included these words:

> In conclusion, be strong in the Lord [be empowered through your union with Him]; draw your strength from Him [that strength which His boundless might provides]. Put on God's whole armor [the armor of a heavy-armed soldier which God supplies], that you may be able successfully to stand up against [all] the strategies and the deceits of the Devil. For we are not wrestling with flesh and blood [contending only with physical opponents], but against the despotisms, against the powers, against [the master spirits who are] the world rulers of this present darkness, against the spirit forces of wickedness in the heavenly (supernatural) sphere. Therefore put on God's complete armor, that you may be able to resist and stand your ground on the evil day [of danger], and, having done all [the crisis demands], to stand [firmly in your place]. Stand therefore [hold your ground], having tightened the belt of truth around your loins and having put on the breastplate of integrity and of moral rectitude and right standing with God, And having shod your feet in preparation [to face the enemy with the firm-footed stability, the promptness, and the readiness produced by the good news] of the Gospel of peace. Lift up over all the [covering] shield of saving faith, upon which you can quench all the flaming missiles of the wicked [one]. And take the helmet of salvation and the sword that the Spirit wields, which is the Word of God.
>
> —Ephesians 6:10–17, AMP

John also told me he saw angels. He said they had once interrupted a satanic ceremony he had attended, and he told me that it frustrated him. It reminded me once again that God is in control and that prayer works.

At the time we met, John was trying to distance himself from these practices, but those involved weren't letting him go. Even in prison they would attempt to intimidate him and demonstrate their influence. The prison scanned all incoming and outgoing mail, but somehow letters written in blood still made their way to John. Yet he was still relatively safer inside the walls of the correctional center, even with all of its darkness and evil.

During my four months of work at the prison, I discovered that approximately one-third of the staff and prisoners had some kind of active affiliation with the occult. At the end of my internship there, I felt relieved to be completing my involvement with the darker side of the human condition. I held onto the few and miraculous victories I had witnessed, but I was ready to move on. Little did I know that this was just the training camp for what I was about to experience.

In a move toward what I thought would be the other end of the spectrum, I applied for and was accepted into an internship with a Christian counseling clinic. I don't know exactly whom I expected to be counseling, but I was in for a shock. During this internship, I would see many clients who were diagnosed with dissociative identity disorder and had survived satanic ritual abuse.

Despite my educational preparation and having a great internship supervisor, I felt unprepared to take on such clients. So I read case files, attended seminars and gathered all the information I could. This internship would challenge me to dig into the Bible like never before to gain a deeper understanding of spiritual warfare. Seeing what I saw and knowing what I now know has forever changed me. A level of innocence is gone. Ritual abuse, whether performed by a religious psychopath, a pedophile, or a serial sadist, has its roots in the darkest places of hell.

Early in the internship, I met a young woman who taught me what it truly means to be a survivor. She was a living testimony that God's grace is sufficient. In 2 Corinthians 12:9 the Lord told Paul, "My grace is sufficient for you, for my strength is made perfect in weakness," and with that verse in mind, I chose the alias "Grace" for this woman I'm about to tell you about. She took me inside her world—a place that was foreign to me and one that would stretch my faith in new ways. I learned the tactics of Satan and the vulgar things he does to try to separate people from the love of Christ. I promised Grace that I would tell people her incredible story. She knew there would be those who would still not believe it, but she felt the information needed to be shared so other survivors could get help.

At birth, Grace was dedicated as a satanic bride. She was trained in the ways of the occult and experienced unspeakable kinds of torture before the age of six. I'm not going to go into the details of her torture, but I'll say this: On September 18, 1992, Governor Jim Edgar of Illinois signed Public #87-1167, allowing for the definition, investigation and prosecution of ritual crimes occurring against children in Illinois. The law includes sacrifices, threatening of bodily harm or death, and other inhumane behaviors forced on a child. Grace experienced every one of the tortures listed in this law, short of death.

Grace's coping mechanism was to dissociate as she endured both mental and physical abuse. She would "go" somewhere else or become someone else. I believe those who survive such horrible experiences do so because they have an extremely creative and brilliant mind. Grace was always thinking, evaluating and analyzing on a conscious and subconscious level.

Grace first ended up in therapy after she realized the horror that existed in her life and attempted to commit suicide. She was found standing in the middle of a busy street. While in therapy, and even afterward, she had to hide from her family. They were constantly trying to find her and bring her back to the occult.

I would pray with Grace before and after our sessions. The Holy Spirit helped and directed me as her therapist. I discovered that I could rely on God to continuously direct me each step of the way in order to best assist in her healing process.

Grace had an amazing sense of humor and often made me laugh. At other times, it would take everything I had to keep from breaking down when she shared her memories. Sometimes Grace would dissociate into one of her "child" parts, and we would then have to delve into the past when she was abused as a child. This was especially difficult for me as a therapist. I knew she was experiencing the pain and torture all over again, yet it was critical for us to go back in time and return to those moments.

I had Grace walk through the memories and picture Jesus with her. He gave her the strength to overcome. After one of these therapy sessions, I couldn't resist crying after she told me what had happened to her when she was six years old. (I don't feel this information would be appropriate to include in this book, because it would simulate a scene from a horror movie.) I thought I had messed up as a therapist and apologized to my supervisor and mentor, Dr. Mitsch, for breaking down. He reassured me and told me that I wouldn't be human if I had been able to hear such horror and not have some sort of reaction.

The fact that Grace survived was literally a miracle. While she was being tortured, her abusers told her that God was responsible for her punishment. They told her that Jesus hated her. Yet, in the end, His love prevailed. His light helped her overcome the intense darkness she had experienced. She began to feel His love and grow in it.

After my internship was over, Grace and I kept in touch for a long time. This is a rare thing to do with a client, but this case was unique and I wanted her to let my supervisor and me know how she was doing. She eventually married and had children of her own. Unfortunately, she frequently moved to prevent her parents from finding her, and we eventually lost contact.

People have often asked how I could have worked with survivors of the occult. The answer is that God sustained me. My husband and children have also always been my best therapy. They provided a wonderful outlet that included love, support and much laughter. I have been blessed with friends and family who encouraged me to move forward in the ministry. I had no previous experience with people diagnosed with dissociative identity disorder or who had survived satanic ritual abuse, and through this experience I learned about a whole new world. It is a chaotic, hurtful and horrifying place. I can only pray that I brought some organization, hope, healing and peace into the lives of those I touched through God's grace.

As a Christian, this experience deepened my faith. It forced me (in a good way) to challenge my understanding of an ever-loving Father. It helped me to realize that God allows for free will and that sometimes people make poor choices. He helped me to pity those who chose darkness—despite the desire, in my flesh, to hate them for the abuses they perpetrated on children and others. In a way, I think these people have dissociated as well by becoming individuals who no longer feel the pain of separation from the love of God. The concept of not knowing His love is unfathomable to me.

The enemy is not imaginary. He is not a little red cartoon character with horns and a pitchfork. He literally seeks to kill, steal and destroy. He is a master of manipulation and knows our every weakness. We are to be aware of him but not to fear him, for we have all the weapons necessary to defeat him through Christ.

> Everyone has heard about your obedience, so I am full of joy over you; but I want you to be wise about what is good, and innocent about what is evil. The God of peace will soon crush Satan under your feet. The grace of our Lord Jesus be with you.
>
> —Romans 16:19–20

Chapter 8

Blessed Be His Name

Legacy of Two Mothers

Once there were two women who never knew each other.
One, my darling, is your birth mom and the other is your mother.
Two different lives, shaped to make yours one.
One became your guiding star; the other became your sun.
The first gave you life, and the second taught you to live it.
The first gave you a need for love, and the second was there to give it.
One gave you a nationality; the other gave you a name.
One gave you the seed of talent; the other gave you aim.
One gave you emotions; the other calmed your fears.
One saw your first sweet smile; the other dried your tears.
One chose adoption. It was all that she could do.
The other prayed for a child, and God led her straight to you.
And now you ask me through your tears,
The age-old question through the years.
Heredity or environment, which are you the product of?
Neither, my darling, neither. Just two different kinds of love.

—Author unknown

It's funny how one phone conversation can change your life. Nancy called me one day early in 1995. She had become a very close friend during the years following Elizabeth's ordeal. She was calling to tell me about a baby girl who had been born with half of a heart. The baby had been placed for adoption, but the adoptive couple had heard about the disability and backed out. The baby was a couple weeks old and was recovering from her first open-heart surgery. She would soon be well enough to leave the hospital, but she had nowhere to go.

Jim and I had been talking about adopting a child with special needs. We already knew the ins and outs of caring for a baby with medical issues. I knew without a doubt that we had to take her in. Jim knew, too. His comment was that everything we had been through with Elizabeth would have been wasted if we didn't step up now.

Jim and I knew that getting involved meant we faced the possibility of losing another child. This fact was not lost on many of those who were close to us, either, and they voiced their concerns. We listened but held to our decision. In the end, we believed it would be worth giving this precious child a quality of life for as long as possible.

I called Nancy back and told her we wanted to meet the baby. We arrived at the hospital two hours later. We walked up to the pediatric unit, and there she was. She had the biggest, most beautiful brown eyes. It was love at first sight. She was in a swing by the nurses' station, because apparently they had fallen in love with her as well. They led us to a private room where I was able to sit and hold her. She looked at me, reached up, and then brushed her hand against my face. My heart melted and our bond was solidified. Many people ask me if it was different from holding a child I'd given birth to, and I can honestly and emphatically answer, "Absolutely not!" She became my child.

We named her Nichole, which means "victorious heart."

A few weeks later, she had recovered enough to come home with us. During that time, we had to overcome some hurdles of our own. We met with the counselor from the adoption agency and were told that it was necessary for us to have an open adoption due to the complexity of the medical situation. In preparation of this, we were interviewed, our house was inspected, and a mountain of paperwork was signed.

It would be the beginning of all sorts of trials and tribulations that we would encounter on the path to giving Nikki a good home. I won't go into all of the details, but the basic problem was this: During the foster care period, the adoption agency was Nikki's legal guardian. They collected her welfare and disability payments and made her medical decisions, but when the time came they were resistant to assigning guardianship without signing a contract that would still enable them to receive the welfare checks. That led to a legal battle involving the Illinois Department of Children and Family Services and the district state's attorney. Long delays were inevitable. We learned the adoption agency had been brought to court many times prior to our situation. In the meantime, thankfully, the hospital and cardiology group were very generous and helped us make sure Nikki received the care she needed.

During this same time period, our son Josh, who had just turned one year old, began to have seizures—sometimes as many as three per day. Doctors diagnosed him with a rather rare condition that kids usually outgrow, so we just had to watch and prevent him from choking, falling or otherwise hurting himself during an episode. Nikki also required constant monitoring and medications that we administered at two-hour intervals around the clock. But through it all, Jimmie, Josh and Nikki were developing a tight bond.

Between the stress of the delayed adoption process and the physical demands at home, my own health began to deteriorate. Then I discovered I was pregnant again—which was a true blessing, but also a wake-up call, because it was no longer just my health that was being affected. Trying to maintain my sanity and energy as the morning sickness progressed to an all-day sickness was a serious challenge. I was exhausted.

In the fall of 1995, Jim accepted a position as a clinical physician at Palmer College of Chiropractic. This was a good opportunity for us and would provide needed financial stability to our situation. The cardiologists approved the move to Iowa, but the adoption agency wasn't as cooperative. They refused to let Nikki leave Illinois. Jim had to start the job, so he shared an apartment with a friend of ours and came home on the weekends.

It was during this period of time that I made plans to meet Nancy for dinner one weekday night. I got lost on the way to the restaurant and stopped at another restaurant to ask for directions. I had my three kids in the car, so I parked by the entrance and planned to ask for directions from the first person I saw. When a woman walked by, I said, "Excuse me . . ."

As soon as she turned in my direction, I gasped. I recognized the eyes immediately. They were Nikki's. I shook it off, got the directions, and turned to go back to the car. But I couldn't leave without finding out if this woman was somehow related to Nikki. I knew Nikki's mother's last name, so I caught up with the woman and asked her if that was her last name.

"No," she said. "But my daughter's is."

The woman was Nikki's grandma. When I told her my last name, her mouth dropped open. I asked her if she would like to meet her granddaughter. Her eyes widened, and she put her hand to her mouth and nodded. We walked over to the car, and I brought the children out. I saw the immediate connection between the two. They had the same expressions and movements. It was surreal.

We had a great conversation—one that I hold dear to my heart. When it was time to go, we hugged and cried. I knew this meeting would one day lead to Nikki being reunited with her birth family. I knew it, but I needed time to process it. It was more than I could handle at the moment. Nancy and I had a lot to talk about once I found the restaurant.

While Jim worked in Iowa, our attorney continued to represent us in court, and I added prenatal visits to my schedule. The baby I carried had an abnormal heartbeat, and the doctors' concern added to my stress. Something had to change, and soon. Our prayers were answered, in part, about six weeks later, just before Christmas, when a judge overruled the adoption agency and allowed us to move to Iowa. We were finally together again, and it felt great.

It wouldn't be long, however, before we became acquainted with the local hospital, for just a few weeks later, Josh became dehydrated with a virus and was admitted. Two days later, I was there with him when Jim called and said that he and Nikki were downstairs in the ER. She had something completely different. To limit cross contamination, she was admitted to the room next to Josh's. We had to rely on our new neighbors to watch Jimmie while Jim worked and I ran between hospital rooms.

Josh and Nikki had grown as close as twins, so they knew each other's voices and cries. They called and answered each other from their adjoining rooms. Even though at times I felt like pulling my hair out, I had to laugh. They were released after a couple of days and life returned to normal—or to at least what could be considered normal for us.

One night, all of us were eating dinner at a restaurant when we noticed that an older couple was watching us. We didn't think there was anything especially noteworthy about our family, but obviously they did. When we got up to leave, the couple approached us. I knew they would.

"We can see the resemblance of these two," they said, nodding to our blond-haired boys with fair skin, "but what about her? She doesn't fit in."

Nikki, being part Italian, had big, brown eyes and olive skin. I was amazed at their tactlessness and told them, "It was the mailman." They walked away with a huff. All we could do was shake our heads and laugh.

There was much laughter in our family, and we took great joy in watching the boys teach their baby sister new things during the next two months. Our family continued to grow closer and to love each other more and more. However, it was becoming more and more apparent that Nikki was growing weaker. This was a sign the doctors had warned us about. She needed another surgery. This was disturbing for two reasons: first, because it was one of those eventualities we knew was coming but always hoped would be later rather than sooner; and second, because the adoption agency was still not forthcoming with the releases and payments. As we pursued this round of treatment, they would dig in their heels as hard as ever.

This was life or death, and Jim and I knew we had to call Nikki's birth mom. We knew it was time to tell her everything and brainstorm a possible solution. I thought again and again about the inevitable call, rehearsing what I would say to her so that I wouldn't break down completely on the phone. I went to take a shower before I called, and there I saw the sun shining through the window, forming a rainbow on the wall. It was going to be the hardest call I ever had to make, but

God would provide me with the strength. In the end, we all agreed to meet the next day.

If all went like Jim and I knew it would, we would be giving our baby back to the birth mom in a reverse adoption. I could hardly wrap my mind around that idea, much less sort out the emotions I was feeling.

The next day came, and I saw the same immediate connection between Nikki and her birth mother that I had seen with Nikki and her grandma. It reinforced the premonition that I had felt several months before this reunion. I hurt, but I also felt God's peace. As I recognized that peace and embraced it, I thanked God for His comfort during this time of need. I knew this was His plan for us all and that Nikki would ultimately be safer for it. We talked, and Nikki's birth mom left with some serious thinking to do before we met again at Nikki's next cardiology appointment.

Nikki needed an ultrasound of her heart and I needed one of my baby in utero, so at that next appointment, Nikki's birth mom and grandma took her into one room while I went into the room next door. The doctors had been informed of what was going on and agreed to make the transition as smooth as possible for everyone. The entire cardiology group was saddened by what was going to be a heartbreaking necessity for us and angry at the circumstances that had caused it. Having become our second family, they were also very supportive and understanding.

One of our prayers had been for Nikki to become strong enough to delay that surgery until the transition could take place. The ultrasound confirmed that, miraculously, she had stabilized. The surgery was postponed for two months.

We had also been praying for the baby in my womb. I saw the tears in my doctor's eyes as he gave us the results of the ultrasound. We were having a baby girl, and her heart murmur was gone! God was confirming again that this was His plan. He had everything under control.

Nikki was 15 months old when we did the reverse adoption. The birth mom adopted her own daughter, and we have been blessed to know that she has since taken great care of her. We were there with her for Nikki's next open heart surgery, and we were invited to her birthdays for several years after. At these gatherings, Nikki would place her hand on my cheek. She knew there was some connection, but obviously her memory was fuzzy, and her birth mom chose not to tell her about those first 15 months of her life.

I think of Nikki every day, and she will always have a piece of my heart. She has turned out to be the best-case scenario for a baby born with her condition. I have no doubt that God has great plans for her.

> For He foreordained us (destined us, planned in love for us) to be adopted (revealed) as His own children through Jesus Christ, in accordance with the purpose of His will [because it pleased Him and was His kind intent].
> —Ephesians 1:5, AMP

The following months after the reverse adoption were hard for the boys as well. They missed Nikki, but they were comforted a bit by the promise of another sister who was coming soon. Jessica MacKenzie Clapper was born on her due date a few months later. I wish I could write that the occasion was uneventful, but it was not. At her birth, she coded and was rushed to PICU, déjà vu. She even looked like Elizabeth.

We were confused, because the most recent tests had shown that her heart was fine. We made the phone calls again to people all over the country and asked them to join us in prayer. When I heard that the doctors were thinking of flying Jessica to another hospital, I walked straight into the PICU, picked up her charts, and scanned the test results. One nurse asked me to leave, while another told her I knew what I was doing and that she should let me be. Jim and I prayed right there beside our daughter for a miracle. I knew we were not alone in this prayer, and I felt it. I was bold enough to tell the nurse that Jessica was going to be okay. Within 24 hours, she stabilized. When we were discharged, we drove her straight to the cardiology group. They confirmed that our baby girl did indeed have a healthy heart.

Through this, God not only took care of Jessica but also healed me in a way that I didn't expect. I was still holding guilt in my heart for Elizabeth's condition. People had told me that maybe I hadn't prayed hard enough or said the right words or had enough faith, or that maybe she had been punished for my own sin. Even though I knew these things were untrue, I questioned it as a mother . . . in my heart. Seeing God's hand on the situation and witnessing His miraculous power during Jessica's first hours showed me His providence. Our children are His children. He knows them and has plans for them. He gives and takes away. Either way, He asks us to trust and obey, because the truth is that He is God and we are not.

At the time of writing this book, Jessica is now a beautiful 12-year-old and is full of life! She loves to encourage others and has great compassion. She and I are very close as mother and daughter, and we have had many great memories.

> Naked I came from my mother's womb, and naked I will depart. The LORD gave and the LORD has taken away; may the name of the LORD be praised.
>
> —Job 1:21

Chapter 9

Living Life Daily

I recently spoke with a friend who had just been diagnosed with stage-four cancer. We talked as moms. We cried and prayed. Having experienced a life-threatening illness for seven years and chronic disease all my life, I was able to share the testimonies of what I had seen happen in our children's lives. I explained how our children have learned compassion and caring for others and how they have seen God give them strength during difficult trials.

My friend wept on the other end of the phone line. I wanted to assure her that everything would be fine. I wanted to tell her that she would live and see her children grow up. But I didn't really know if it would be true or not. I prayed for it, but we both knew she could die from the cancer.

A mom needs to be practical, so we begin to plan what needs to be done—"just in case." I know in my own life that I have "my ducks in a row." I have told Jim what my funeral should look like (chocolate and dancing need to be included) and have spoken to him about my hopes for him if I were to leave this world. I have spoken with family and friends about the things I would like my children to know. I have written this book for my children.

The following is a letter I wrote to my kids one night. It explains what I have felt as a mom, and I hope it encourages others who are experiencing illness.

I am writing tonight after I just cried. I am 38 years old now and have been living with this chronic illness all of my life. I never have lied to you kids, and I will not begin now. It is hard at times. I do get tired, but know I will never give up the fight. I do get scared, but then I feel His presence.

When I was a kid, I was in and out of hospitals a lot. Papa Sullivan would joke with me after I got shots that if I drank water, I would be a fountain. He knew how to make me laugh! Grandma Sullivan would cheer me on to get better. Kids made fun of me because I was pale with blue lips. Be thankful for hair gel, because we had none (back in the "olden days") and my hair was a frizzy mess. Yet I learned after watching Star Wars (the one from 1977) that my heavy, labored, breathing mimicked a certain character: Darth Vader. The kids loved it!

I didn't get to go to many birthday parties because, as you are well aware, I cannot be in homes with animals. I didn't attend various field trips, hence, my lack of knowledge about farms (okay, so I didn't know what an "udder" was—cows only said "moo" in the books I read). I could not go out for recess because the weather would affect my breathing. Instead, I stayed inside to help tutor those who were mainstreamed with special needs. They became my friends. It also provided me with a compassion that encouraged me to get into ministry to the disabled when I was older.

You asked me the other day if it hurts to get all the injections I receive. I am accustomed to needles, and sometimes that is a frustrating fact. Other times I get bored of therapy. It seems monotonous, and I wish it would go away. I am thankful for it, though, because it has strengthened me. I have learned much about the body and believe God has allowed me to help others with similar conditions. Good always comes from the "tough" stuff.

I can handle the physical pain, but I worry about being a burden to you and your dad. You've never made me feel that way. I know I am very active overall, but I also know that you know that sometimes I just need to slow down and get some rest.

You have sacrificed not having a dog, and Josh, I know you know every single kind of dog that exists through your persistent studying. Yet not once have you complained. You have realized that I cannot enjoy specific activities with you because my lungs would not handle it. One of the most difficult things for me to handle is to see your expressions when I go into respiratory distress.

Do you remember the time it happened at church? You may remember, James, since you were old enough to remember hearing people say that I was going to die. I did not have enough breath to tell them to be quiet so as not to scare all of you. I could barely say, "I love you." I didn't know if that would be the last time I would see you. I am usually optimistic, but I do realize the danger I am in.

Dad was not yet at the church, and when he got there, he heard that I was in a serious condition. I found out from a friend that when he was getting ready to leave the church to get to the ER, he just stood in the snow for a moment. He does not know I know that, but I know it has been hard for him.

James, you came to the hospital two days after that episode. The nurses were wonderful and let you stay in bed with me. I explained to you my funky oxygen mask and why there was a tube coming out of my arm. You ate lunch with me, and we just cuddled for hours. You were the best medicine! You turned to me and said that you knew Dad didn't like cleaning the showers, and so when you got home, you would clean them. You were such a big boy!

It was hard on you, though, when I contracted a life-threatening illness. You would time me if I left to go anywhere. You were so afraid I was not going to come back and that I would end up in the hospital or die.

Joshua, you expressed it in a different way. You got very quiet. You have made sure through the years that when I am sick, I always had a blanket. You make me the best green tea! You find ways to comfort and serve me.

Jessica, you have made me beautiful cards and gifts. I know how much my condition has scared you, too. There was a moment when you were three when you laid hands on me and started praying out loud for God to heal me. There were family, friends, doctors and nurses around, and none of us were sure if we should laugh at the sweetness or cry because it was so pure.

One time when I was being wheeled into the ER, all of you were crying. My heart broke. I usually drove myself to the ER if I could or got someone else so that Dad could stay with you. This has been critical to me. Dad has been so good at comforting all of you and maintaining calmness through my hospitalizations.

Remember the time I started going into anaphylactic shock while I was driving our van? Thankfully, we were very close to the hospital. James took the phone and was ready to dial 911. Josh and Jess, you both started praying. We were able to contact Granddad and Grandma Clapper, and they met us at the ER. You were all so calm, and I saw how God had given you strength. I also believe your prayers sustained me.

Dad and you give me mental strength. When I feel bad, all I have to do is think of all of you. I want to be here for you for graduations, marriages, grandbabies and so many other future memories.

God has been faithful through it all. When I have been close to dying, I feel an overwhelming peace, and yet I pray that if I am to stay here on earth He would give me the strength to fight. When I need it, I feel an overwhelming energy, and I feel His presence so strongly. It obviously has not been my time, and I am thankful for the time He has given me. I am actually looking forward to celebrating my fortieth birthday! I hope to thank all those who have stood by us through the years.

God has allowed me a little insight into His suffering. I cannot fathom what He endured for us, but I know that I hear Him the best when I am physically exhausted. Perhaps tonight I can write all this because I am so tired. It seems that when I am my weakest and cannot fight so much, that's when God's power really shows up.

I would never have wished any of this on you, and yet I believe lessons have been learned that could only have been learned through experience. I see such compassion in all of you. When we volunteered as a family at the Joni and Friends Disability Family Retreat, each of you excelled in your gifting. You understood struggle.

Josh and Jess, you acted so courageously this past spring when I fainted in the driveway. You handled it with calmness. You were so mature. James, you proved again this summer that you can handle emergency situations when you pushed my wheelchair into the ER. Sometimes I wish that you didn't have to experience such things because of me, because I am supposed to protect you. And yet, I see God in you as you help me. I am so blessed to have the honor of raising you unto Him.

I do believe I will live a long life. If God calls me to heaven sooner than that, then know I am so proud of you and how you have handled all of this. I know He has given you great wisdom and insight that only comes through trials. I appreciate each extra day I have with you.

I love you more than you can imagine,

Mom

And God shall wipe away all tears from their eyes; and there shall be no more death, neither sorrow, nor crying, neither shall there be any more pain: for the former things are passed away.

—Revelation 21:4, KJV

Chapter 10

Inner Beauty

Over the next couple of years, I continued to work as a therapist. Jim was working at his alma mater in chiropractic care, and life was proceeding normally again. My relationship with God was stronger than ever, and I was growing spiritually. I relished my quiet times with Him and was learning to hear His voice. During one of these quiet times, I thought I heard God tell me I was going to work with actors and actresses in Hollywood.

I started laughing. It was such a far-fetched idea. Here I was, a true Chicago girl at heart, living in Iowa, and very far away from California. I remember telling the women at the Bible study I attended about it. I told them my analysis of the situation was that I was just supposed to pray for movie stars. Having worked with youth, I realized the significant impact these actors, actresses and models have on our culture. We all know they could use a little prayer, but this couldn't mean that I would personally interact with them. However, as it turns out, God has a great sense of humor.

While we were living in Iowa, my health took a turn for the worse. I had just contracted chicken pox for the second time in my life. I didn't think it was possible for someone to get the chicken pox twice, but I've accomplished many medical feats that no one thought possible. When I first saw the bumps, I giggled a little, thinking it would be a small case. Boy, was I wrong. It broke out everywhere.

I soaked myself in an oatmeal bath in an attempt to stop the itching. I would lay in such a way that my nose was the only part of my body sticking out of the water. I found the situation to be humorous at first, but that didn't last long. I was not feeling right at all. The situation turned serious. I not only had chicken pox all over my body but also in my throat and lungs.

I ended up in the hospital. We didn't know it at the time, but while I was in the hospital, I contracted another disease called aspergillosis—a life-threatening disease that involves fungus in the lungs. My condition got worse daily. The high levels of mold, dust and bacteria in the air had found their way into my weakened lungs. Three different doctors and specialists told me it would probably be best if I moved to a different climate—preferably somewhere in the western United States.

Jim began looking for jobs in the West, and I began preparing to leave Iowa. This meant saying goodbye to great friends and moving further away from family. Jim got an interview for a job in Denver and was offered a job there—but first he had to train for six months in Southern California.

My friends in Iowa threw me a surprise going-away party. Toward the end of the night, they prayed for me. Unexpectedly, many of us felt a strange sense that I was going on a "mission trip."

Jim and I found a house in Laguna Niguel. I began working with the youth in the area, and they shared many of their school experiences with me. I soon discovered that one of the main issues facing the youth of Orange County was image, primarily due to the fact that they were so close to Hollywood. It was not unheard of for teens to receive plastic surgery as a high school graduation gift. The more insecurity I encountered, the more I wanted to talk to the youth about inner beauty. I was aware that this was a problem many youth faced in America. God put it on my heart to get into the schools in the area and speak on the topic. However, to get into the schools, I first needed to gain some kind of credibility.

After discussing my concern with a few people, I made the decision to enter a pageant that was committed to community, marriage and family. I felt this would give me the necessary "title" I needed to gain access to the schools and speak. At the time, I was on steroids for my lungs, and my face and body were swollen. Nevertheless, I decided to make an interview video and submit it to the pageant. A few weeks later, I received news that I had been awarded the city title. It seemed to be perfect, because I didn't have to go on stage or anything of that sort. I had a mission, and the plans seemed to be coming together. Later that week, however, I received a call from the pageant supervisor informing me that there was indeed going to be an actual pageant event.

I felt like the undercover FBI agent in the movie *Miss Congeniality*. I was a mother who had worked as a therapist in the prison system, and now I was about to wear a rhinestone tiara. Life can be an adventure and, as I've mentioned, God has quite a sense of humor.

I thought my position as the city title-holder was strictly local, but then I received a phone call from officials telling me that all city title-holders, including myself, had to make multiple public appearances. Over the next few weeks, Jim and I attended several celebrity functions in Beverly Hills and Hollywood, and I met up with those same actors and actresses I had been called to pray for back in Iowa. (I could do some name dropping here, but I will refrain from doing so because these celebrities deserve their privacy. Through this pageant experience, I came to see that one of the many downfalls of fame is the tremendous intrusion into these people's personal lives.)

The first event Jim and I went to was in Beverly Hills. Because we were on a tight budget due to my medical bills, I found a dress on sale and wore shoes from a discount shoe store. We stood in line to get into the place until someone realized that I was a title-holder and escorted us to the front. It's interesting how differently you are treated when you are wearing a crown. People approached me and said that I looked "fabulous" and asked which designer did my shoes and gown. When I told them the truth, they looked stunned. In fact, some of them probably thought I was joking.

These people didn't understand that the way you look has an internal factor. This was perhaps most evident in some of the movie stars I saw in attendance. These individuals made a lot of money and were supposed to be so glamorous, but many of them looked to me as though they were going through the motions. They seemed depressed and empty. My interaction with many of them confirmed my initial reaction that fame, beauty and fortune are not the sole ingredients for happiness.

Lots of people came up to me and made comments about the way I looked. Sometimes they were positive. Other times, people felt that they had the right and moral obligation to tell me what I needed to do. For example, one woman told me I needed a nose job (I like my nose, by the way). Another explained that I should have plastic surgery done on my eyes. "Oh darling, I love the dress. It brings out the color of your eyes. Speaking of which [talking in a sad tone now], have you ever thought of a lift? I mean, such a shame to leave them like that." At one of the events at the NBC studios, a man asked me if I should really be eating a hamburger. Wasn't it bad for a "beauty queen" to eat like that?!

Yet for all the negative comments I endured, I also received positive remarks from women and young girls who thanked me for being real. They were excited to see that a person could wear a crown and still be authentic. I enjoyed being able to encourage other women about their body image and about who they were both inside and out. I especially loved being able to speak to teens.

Not too long after that, Jim and I were the host and hostess at a birthday party for a famous celebrity realtor at a penthouse in Beverly Hills. After wishing this woman a happy birthday, she looked at me and told me there was something different about me and she thought it was beautiful. I really believe this was because she saw Jesus in me. She went on to tell me that she only knew a couple of people at the party and that the rest were all there for publicity. She seemed so lonely.

Jim and I mingled for a while, talking to all kinds of "important" people. There were directors, producers, actors, actresses, hairdressers to the stars, and plenty of wannabes. The wannabes carried around envelopes that contained headshots, business proposals, resumes, and other items to get them noticed. Everything in these circles is a networking opportunity.

I met a woman who had been a famous actress in the 70s. She gave me her "resume" by verbally going through her accomplishments and insisted that a group of us join her for dinner that night. She said she knew the manager at a four-star restaurant and that we could get prime rib and shrimp cocktail for 10 dollars a piece. We were hungry and the

Velveeta cheese squares and cocktail weenies at the party had long since disappeared, so we accepted the invitation.

We got the directions and agreed to meet the rest of the group inside the restaurant. When we got there, we were surprised to discover that the place had a basement—a rare thing in earthquake-prone California. When we went down the stairs, Jim and I noticed some interesting posters of scantily clothed women. As we descended, I saw the pole. Yes, we were in a strip bar.

The first thought that came to mind was, *Great, I can just see tomorrow's newspaper headlines: "Colleen Clapper, Homeschool Mom, Youth Leader and Pageant Title-holder, Dies in Basement of Strip Club During Earthquake."* Still, I am always up for unconventional ministry, and I knew there was a reason for my being there. Besides, if Jesus socialized and ate with people from all walks of life, why shouldn't I?

As it turned out, I was able to minister to our waitress. I saw her disposition and knew she was hurting. Whenever she looked at me, I saw pain in her eyes. I began writing messages on my napkins to give to her. I wrote about how she had great worth and that Jesus loved her unconditionally. By the way she responded, squeezing my hand as she took the note, I knew that I was right on track. I don't know what happened to her after I left the club, but I knew she was the reason I had been there.

The next assignment I went to was an awards event in Hollywood. It was a red carpet event and everything, and many famous people were in attendance. There wasn't supposed to be any alcohol served, but that didn't stop some of the attendees from drinking. There seemed to be an understood and generally accepted policy of BYOB. A very well-known actress and her friends passed around a bottle of alcohol under their chairs—taking not-so-discreet swigs in turn. I felt like I was at a prom.

The image these people portray on the screen or on television is so different from the way they are in real life. What I saw was extremely unglamorous. The actress passing around the bottle ended up winning an award and was expected to give a speech. She made her way up on stage, stumbled, and almost fell off. Her words were somewhat scrambled, and with a wink and a nod, she had to be escorted back to her chair. I saw the event on TV a few months later and appreciated anew the skill of an editing team.

Behind the scenes, it is all very different than what we are led to believe. It's not all beautiful. I found it interesting that a photographer at the event came up to me and, not unlike the actress whose birthday I attended, told me I was one of the most beautiful people he had ever seen. I don't feel I am "magazine cover" material, but this man said there was something that glowed inside of me. Again, I believe he saw Jesus in me.

The state pageant was held a few months later. I had already met the other contestants, and we had a lot of fun the week prior to the main event. We went to Disney's California Adventure, to restaurants, to Newport Beach for shopping, and to other places. We were even interviewed by a television station about our opinions on being married women. These women were talented, and most of them were down to earth. It was not difficult to become friends with them. Most really did possess both inner and outer beauty. I really grew to care for them and to appreciate all their gifts and abilities.

I remember at one point, though, that we needed to take off our crowns. Believe it or not, when I went to retrieve mine, it had been taken because it was a "newer" crown, and I received in exchange an "older" crown with rhinestones that had tarnished due to hairspray and other elements. It amazed me just how much these crowns meant to some people. They were beautiful, but they would not last forever. I was reminded that our earthly crowns fade, but that the crowns we receive in heaven are eternal.

My dress was not pageant style—which a couple of contestants quickly pointed out to me. I didn't even know the protocol. I was glad this pageant focused more on community involvement and an interview than on outer beauty. During the interview, I spoke honestly from my heart, and I really felt God's presence. I know there were many people praying for me. Their prayers were not about my winning, but rather about God using me to do His will. I didn't care about winning or losing; I just wanted to be obedient and not waste the opportunity.

The judges asked about my goals, the changes I believed needed to be made in our culture, and about how I could represent married women. I was transparent and real in my answers—no "world peace" clichés from me. Being onstage was difficult for me. We had to parade around in exercise outfits, and with 40 members of the youth group from my church in attendance, it was a bit unnerving. I also had family (including our children) and friends in the audience. I knew that the youth and my family and friends were all praying, and for that I was very thankful.

My favorite part of the event was when Jim escorted me onstage while a speech he had written about me was read. I was so moved by what he wrote that I literally forgot some of the choreography I was supposed to do.

In the end, I guess it was God's will for me to win the pageant. It was crazy. I was very honored. I also knew right away that this was an open door for ministry. I had already been able to witness to people and pray for them, but I knew more experiences were to come and more would be expected of me. Our children joined Jim and me onstage. One of the members of the original *American Gladiators* was present, as were some of the cast of *Baywatch*. A few of the judges teared up (in a good way) at some of the answers I gave during the interview. Now they were playing with James, Josh and Jessica. Family and friends greeted me. The youth group came up onstage. Then I was whisked away for interviews into a special room. My feet hurt and I was exhausted, but I was exhilarated at the same time. The whole experience was quite surreal.

Once you receive a state title, the next step is to participate in an international pageant. There was a website that listed all of the contestants, and I felt as if I were being led to pray daily for each one. I was not in this to win. I really wanted to encourage these women. I was 5' 2", with brown curly hair and a Chicago accent, and I held a pageant title in California. It all seemed so ironic, but I have learned that God can place you anywhere if you are open to His leading.

One of the first requirements was to give a speech in front of all the other contestants. We were supposed to introduce ourselves and talk about the charity we represented—mine was the Make a Wish

Foundation. Instead, I felt God nudge me to also tell them that I had been praying for them.

I had butterflies in my stomach when it was my turn to speak. I wasn't sure how the contestants would receive it, but I knew I had to tell them. As I walked up to the front, I felt this overwhelming sense of love and peace. I felt God's presence. I looked out at all of them and saw such incredible beauty. Many of these women were models, beautiful people physically, but this was different. I believe God allowed me to see them in the same way He does—or at least He gave me a glimpse.

I did my best to express myself to the women, and some of them began to cry. This was not the kind of crying you see in pageants where they fan their hands over their faces—I'm talking about real tears. This opened the door for me to minister. Some of the women were already Christians, and we prayed together. There were others who hadn't really grasped the whole concept of Christianity, and they had many questions. I was able to share the unconditional love of Jesus with them as well.

All of the women were talented and amazing, each in their own unique way. As I spent time with these women, I learned that surgical enhancement is not uncommon in the pageant system. It concerned me that in spite of their natural beauty and talent, a few women still felt the need to take it a step or two further. Two husbands spoke to me and said that their wives had undergone multiple plastic surgeries but still felt dissatisfied. They wished their wives would stop their addiction to the procedure. The struggle in our society to be perfect was in evidence at this gathering.

I was reminded of a striking contrast I had witnessed when I worked with children who had disabilities. One little girl loved to dance, and she would spin and spin around. She had a humble confidence about her, and you couldn't help but be amazed by her charismatic personality. She would look in the mirror and just smile. Some people do that because of vanity, but I never sensed that in her. It seemed as if she just knew how wonderfully she was created. The ironic thing was that she didn't display beauty as defined by our culture.

She had hair growing out from all over her face. One of her eyes was diagonal from the other and her mouth was contorted—even after multiple reconstructive surgeries. I watched as she wrapped a purple silk scarf around herself while dancing, oblivious to everyone. I envied such a simplistic yet profound understanding of beauty. After a while, she turned around and gave me a wonderfully lopsided smile. *This,* I thought to myself, *is true beauty, both inside and outside.* I found myself wishing that some of these contestants could look into the mirror and see themselves just like that little dancing girl had seen herself.

Although I have not struggled a lot with my own self-image, I do get self-conscious when I have to go back on steroids for my lungs. The steroids add pounds fast—I can gain 20 to 30 pounds within a few weeks. My face becomes bloated, and I look even paler than I naturally am. In fact, at the time of writing this book, my metabolism is really messed up, and I cannot get the swelling down because I have been on steroids for so long. Thankfully, I have an amazing husband who finds me beautiful and sexy no matter what. This helps me a great deal during these times, and I am saddened that not all husbands are like Jim.

But maybe things are starting to change. I have noticed lately that models of all sizes are being used in various advertisements. In addition, I recently watched a dance show in which one of the participants was not stick-thin. She radiated beauty. We need role models for our youth who will show that it is okay to be who they are and not try to change themselves drastically to please others. It's not wrong for a person to want to do things to improve his or her health, but it is a concern when it becomes an obsession or an addiction. I hope the trend continues to change.

When I lived in California, I encountered a woman who exuded incredible confidence. I first saw her when she was exiting a store, and I thought she was gorgeous. She had the most brilliant blue eyes and white hair. She had wrinkles all over her face and amazing smile lines. She had a rounded body shape, and she seemed to have energy to spare. Still, she was gentle in her spirit. I stopped her and asked her what her "secret" was. She said that she prayed and found true joy in God. She also told me that she was 80 years old. I hope I look like that when I am 80!

> Charm and grace are deceptive, and beauty is vain [because it is not lasting], but a woman who reverently and worshipfully fears the Lord, she shall be praised!
>
> —Proverbs 31:30, AMP

Chapter 11

Generation to Generation

Fear not [there is nothing to fear], for I am with you; do not look around you in terror and be dismayed, for I am your God. I will strengthen and harden you to difficulties, yes, I will help you; yes, I will hold you up and retain you with My [victorious] right hand of rightness and justice.

—Isaiah 41:10, AMP

Not long after the events of September 11, 2001, Jim and I knew that it was time to move back to Illinois because my health began to decrease further. Prior to that, both my great-grandma and a close friend had passed away, and because I was in California, I was not able to attend their funerals. I was ready to go back home to Illinois where both of our families lived. I felt as though God was releasing us from His ministry in California. Ministry is never really ours. It is God's, and He is quite capable of assigning it to whomever He wants. It was a privilege to be involved, but I was looking forward to relaxing safely at home in Illinois. I was not prepared for what was about to happen next.

It December 2001, we were finally home sweet home. I anxiously ran up to my dad to give him a hug, only to have shivers run down my spine. I had this awful feeling and knew God was allowing me to gain insight. I felt Him say in His quiet voice that something was wrong and that I needed to pray. By now, I was pretty familiar with this feeling. God has often allowed me to *know* when big things are going to happen for the purpose of interceding for the person.

Two days later, my brother called to tell me that my father had been in for some tests and that the tests were showing he had a lump in his lungs. He had cancer, and doctors feared it had spread to his bones. I was devastated, but knew I was supposed to fight on my knees. It turned out to be prostate cancer. My dad had to go through radiation treatment and two angioplasties. My relaxing homecoming was turning into anything but. Yet I wouldn't have wanted to be anywhere else.

About a year went by, and I was reading a book by Charles Swindoll titled *Paul* in which he writes about the shock of losing loved ones in an accident. My family experienced that when my Uncle Tom died in a motorcycle accident and when my Uncle David died when a train hit his car. As a little girl, I had watched one of my friends being placed in an ambulance after being hit by a car. He died a few days later. Each incident was heart wrenching. As I read the book, I thanked God for sparing the rest of our family any recent tragic moments. That night, however, I had a strange nightmare in which I saw members of my family spinning around and around. I was not sure what to make of it, but it was terrifying enough to wake me up.

My brother called the next evening. In a very quiet voice, he told me that our mom and maternal grandma had been in a car accident. This couldn't be happening. I had just been praising God for sparing our family from this kind of trial. My legs went weak, and I felt as if I were going to pass out. I sensed that this was not just a minor accident but that it was something very serious. I knew I had no choice but to pull myself together and find out the details.

Within the hour, we learned that my mom, both my maternal and paternal grandmas, and my aunt had been in the accident. They had been visiting another of my aunts who had just undergone a radical hysterectomy and were driving home when their car was hit and flipped over six times. An oncoming semi-truck had just missed crushing the car. They had been going east, but ended up in the westbound lane. All four women were brought to four different hospitals due to their critical injuries. The accident ended up all over the Chicago news. Helicopters came in, and the jaws of life were used to extract them from the wreckage. Traffic was stopped for more than two hours.

Both of my brothers and all of our spouses drove 45 minutes to Rockford, Illinois, where the accident had occurred. We called the hospitals to find out where we should go first. We wanted to see our mom, but we were told that my grandma had sustained the greatest injuries and that she was in surgery. She was also receiving multiple blood transfusions. With the medical background I have, I was able to ask specific questions, and I quickly realized that we had to get to her first. We found out that her head had hit the dashboard and that she had sustained massive trauma. She was still alive when we reached the hospital, but she was in critical condition.

Grandma and I had always been very close. Just the week before, I had been resting on the couch, not feeling well, and she had placed a blanket on me. She had always comforted me as a child. I always knew I could go to her for anything. We had also just gone to see the movie *My Big Fat Greek Wedding* with my mom because my grandma was half Greek. She had passed down a lot of her Greek heritage to me. Before the accident, I had been rummaging through a box of mementos and found a book that she had given me when I was little. The book was about God, and I was going to have her read it to my children. I never would have imagined that only a few days from then my family and I would be in a waiting room, holding each other and crying as we had to let her go.

Grandma Heron died shortly after arriving in the operating room. The coroner asked for someone to identify her body. I knew someone needed to do it, because decisions had to be made for the funeral. I would have to decide on an open or closed casket. I was familiar with the protocol, having made plans for our daughter. I also was still in disbelief that this was happening. It shouldn't be like this.

I went into the room where they had laid her body. Jim came with me, for which I was grateful. As I entered the room, my knees began to give. I went over and touched my grandma's hand for the last time. Her beautifully manicured hand was the only way I could identify her. She always took great care of her hands and feet. My grandma's favorite memory of me was me wrapping my tiny hand around her index finger. I did it one last time.

It turned out that the nurse in the room with us knew our family. She said she had been praying for my grandma in the surgery room. I knew she was praying for us, too, because I felt an overwhelming peace in the room. She handed me my grandma's purse, and I took one of the IDs out. I just needed to hold onto something of hers. To this day, I still have her ID in my purse, and I look at it often to remember how she would wear this certain color of lipstick and have her hair just right. I also listen to a tape she made for me of her playing the piano and humming the words. This has comforted me during some hard times.

I filled out the paperwork and, as I was doing so, the coroner told me that the man who hit the car was extremely concerned. I learned that he, along with others, had ran to come to the aid of these women. I knew that strangers had been praying, because all my strength had to have come from God that night.

Next, we went to see my mom. The hospitals had contacted each other, and the staff was ready to escort us to the ICU and help direct us to the surgeons and physicians. I was so glad for their help, because we were all still a bit disoriented.

At the time of the accident, they had found my mom with her head pressed to the street. The car was in shreds all around her. They had assumed she was dead, but then she had replied, "Not me! I am not going yet!" They had quickly cut her out of the car, and a helicopter had flown her to the hospital. She had been taken to the ICU, where the first CAT showed that her brain was hemorrhaging. She had a serious head wound with multiple contusions. Her muscles and ligaments along the entire right side of her body had been sprained and strained. The neurologist told me that she was in critical condition. I signed medical papers, giving the doctors permission to do brain surgery or whatever else was needed to keep her alive. No daughter should ever have to experience that. I needed my mom to survive. I couldn't lose her.

The first time I walked in to see her, my heart stopped when I saw the blood and the area where her hair had been scraped off her scalp by the pavement. Her face was swollen, yet she managed to smile at my brothers, our spouses and me.

My dad was in Ohio when the accident occurred. He was supposed to have been on a relaxing golf trip before undergoing another angioplasty, but instead, the next months would be some of the most stressful he would ever endure. We were finally able to contact him at 3:00 in the morning. He drove straight to Illinois and was there the next morning.

Jim and the rest of my family went home, and I stayed with my cousin Jean. Jean and I have gone through many tough times together, and it felt good to have her there. Together, we have developed the ability to find laughter even in the gloomiest of situations. We shared tears that night, but we would also find ourselves in a unique situation. While we were in my mom's ICU room, the fire alarm went off. Sure enough, the nurse came in and closed the glass door for our protection. We couldn't believe it. We were locked in the room. It was like Murphy's Law—whatever can go wrong will.

Jean and I began to come up with outrageous plans on how we were going to lower my mom through the window with hospital sheets and climb down after her. (Of course, we were wearing sensible shoes, unlike so many women in movies with the high heels attempting to escape danger.) Thank God, the fire didn't get far. Later, Jean left, and I was alone with my mom.

We decided not to tell mom about my grandma, as it was absolutely necessary for her to preserve her strength. I dreaded the moment I would have to tell her. As critical as her condition was, she was still concerned for everyone else. I kept answering her questions about her mom, her mother-in-law and her sister-in-law by saying, "they are all peaceful." I didn't want to lie to her, but I also wasn't ready for her to know the whole story.

Mom began to talk to me in the early hours of the morning. She recalled the half scream of her mother and the silence that had followed. The time had come to tell her. As she looked at me, I could see in her eyes that she already knew. She said in a childlike voice that I had never heard before, "My mommy is gone." As I witnessed the pained look on her face at that moment, I silently begged God not to take her too. She couldn't cry without feeling extreme pain. She closed her eyes, and I wrapped my hand around hers. The only sound that could be heard was the constant hum of the monitors.

Mom would later ask me about my paternal grandma. I told her that she had to have two fingers amputated and had sustained a head injury. I also shared that when I had walked into the ICU, the first thing Grandma Sullivan had said was, "Colleen, I was praying the whole time." She was concerned for everyone else and expressed the unselfish love of a mom. As weak as she was, I could feel her strength as she clasped my hand. My grandma was 89 years old at the time and suffered from osteoporosis. She should not have made it, but I knew that God was not quite ready to take her home. We needed this prayer warrior. I knew that her prayers were heard, and that even though things didn't all make sense, we were being held in God's hands.

We were not able to get to the hospital that my aunt was in that night, but I was so thankful that her sister, the one who had just had surgery, was able to be with her. My aunt had cracked ribs and a broken hip. When I spoke with her on the phone, I heard determination in her voice and knew that she would be okay.

I went home and began helping to plan my maternal grandma's funeral. I knew what she would have wanted, because she had just planned her own mother's (my great-grandma's) funeral a year earlier. I took the book I had found just a week before she passed away and quoted the same words on her funeral pamphlet that I had hoped she would read to my children. Miraculously, my mom was able to attend. The funeral home was packed, and we were overwhelmed by the outpouring of love that people showed us.

In the following weeks, I ran back and forth between seven different hospitals as the three women were transferred to different places for their recovery. Now it was my turn to take care of these amazing women who had exemplified to me the various qualities that a mom should possess. These were the women who had mentored me through the years and given me traditions to be passed down. As I went from hospital to hospital, I recalled the many times that all five generations of women had been together. Even as I write this, a smile is on my lips as I think of the crazy times we have had.

A couple of years ago, our family made a kick line with my great-grandma on one end of the line, my grandma and mom in the middle, and me holding my daughter at the other end of the line.

Five generations of women doing our Greek dancing! Memories and prayers carried me through. I realized what a great responsibility it was for me to continue to mentor my daughter in the way that these women had mentored me.

The three women were able to return home after their hospitalizations. My parent's house looked like a hospital ward, complete with therapeutic beds and other medical supplies. Each of the women required physical therapy. Their progress was amazing. My mother received more than 20 bouquets of flower arrangements during the first couple of days she was back home. Hundreds of cards poured in, as well as many meals. Yet what meant the most were the prayers. We needed God's strength.

I will never forget helping my mom with her first shower after the accident. I felt so bad for her as we tried to wash the blood and gravel from her body. My mother must have known how I was feeling. She joked with me about her new hairdo. I marveled at her strength, and I continue to do so. Four months later, she gave her testimony at a church retreat. She talked about miracles and answers to prayers. She continued to give of herself.

Another aunt flew in to help, and she ended up suffering a heart attack. It was such a crazy time. I lived at my house and at my parent's house to help aid in my mom's, my aunt's, and grandma's recovery, and I even had to homeschool our children in hospital waiting rooms. (These were important life lessons for all of us).

At one point during their recovery, a few of us were sitting at the kitchen table. We talked—my grandma, my mom and my aunt, who had been in the accident; my other aunt, who had just had a heart attack; and another aunt, who had been diagnosed with Lyme's Disease; and myself, who had a lung disease. As we looked around at one another, we started laughing. We were one pathetic group! Thank God for the laughter. Thank God we could go through it as a family.

The time came for my mom and me to visit my grandma's gravesite. My grandma was buried next to my daughter, just like she had wanted to be. My mom and I held each other's hands and laid pink roses on Elizabeth's grave, just as we had done 12 years ago. We then placed African violets next to my grandmother's grave, which were her favorite. We stood there with tears streaming down our faces in silence. Our hands clasped one another's, and our grip tightened. No words were necessary.

About a year after the accident, when the pace of life began to slow down, my health began to worsen. My immune system was again shot, and testing showed that my condition was equivalent to a person who had AIDS or cancer. I went to a Christian clinic in Oklahoma, and there God worked miracles. After returning home, I had to continue a regimen that included inducing fever to rid myself of the toxic effects of the thousands of milligrams of steroids that had been used to combat the lung disease.

While I was resting with an induced fever, I heard God say that I was going to be asked to speak about "inner beauty" at a church, and that the talk would lead to my heart's desire. I thought perhaps I was hallucinating. But then, the next day, an area church called and asked me to speak about inner beauty. A woman named Joyce was in attendance. Joyce called me afterward and said she had heard me speak and wondered if I would be interested in doing some ministry.

I found myself at Moody Bible Institute in Chicago, watching a video of Anne Graham Lotz speaking. This was it! This was my heart's cry. All the brokenness would be worth it if I could assist in praying for revival! I was going to be part of an event called "Just Give Me Jesus." My Great-grandpa Pickering, a pastor, had been part of the Chicago revival in the early 1900s. His son, my Grandpa Pickering, had continually prayed for God to raise up another descendent with a heart for Chicago ministry. I knew this was part of a generational blessing. I didn't have to wait long to receive confirmation.

I was distracted at points during the meeting. The very next day was the one-year anniversary of the accident, and I was struggling with not having been able to thank the many strangers whom I had heard had prayed at the scene of the accident. I was also struck by the familiarity I sensed in Judy, another member of the "Just Give Me Jesus" committee. Judy was feeling the same connection, and we started to question each other about where we could have met. She mentioned that her husband was a surgeon at a Rockford hospital. The connections began. Her husband had been my grandma's surgeon that night. Then I found out that Judy had been at the site of the accident! She had watched and prayed as members of my family were taken in helicopters to the various hospitals.

Two other women who overheard our conversation introduced themselves and said they had been at the scene of the accident as well! I was able to thank Judy and the two women from Rockford. My mom was able to thank these women at a later time. God is not a God of coincidences but of amazing surprises.

There was one more thing I needed to do for closure. I had forgiven the driver who had hit the car, but I knew I would eventually need to contact him. I had heard at various times that he was a good man, and for that I was thankful. I knew his life had profoundly changed in a split second and that he had to live with the situation in a completely different way. I was able to contact this man through e-mail and express forgiveness. My mom was able to do the same. I know that it was only through Jesus' grace that we were able to do that.

You should know that my family is not perfect! No family is. But going through difficult times helps one to realize the good things a person has. Everyone has different personalities and various character quirks, and yet each person has something valuable to offer.

I won't even assume to know your family situation, but I pray that there will be testimonies, traditions and memories that you'll be able to pass on to the next generation. If you don't have that kind of a family, then I hope you are the one to start the testimonies, traditions and memories!

> Great is the LORD and most worthy of praise; his greatness
> no one can fathom. One generation will commend your
> works to another; they will tell of your mighty acts.
> —Psalm 145:3–4

Epilogue

Then I heard the voice of the Lord, saying, "Whom shall I send? And who will go for us?" And I said, "Here am I. Send me!"

—Isaiah 6:8

Since the accident, there have been other trials. A few years ago, the kids and I were in our van going down our inclined driveway when the brakes decided to not work. I had to hit our home to stop the van and prevent us from rolling down the hill. The van broke through the bricks and missed the electric box by six inches. Psalm 91:11, "for He shall give His angels charge over you," became very real to us.

In the summer of 2005, Jim was diagnosed with a cyst that had to be surgically removed immediately. In the spring of 2007, Josh had a serious form of mono. James was just hospitalized a few weeks ago. I'm pleased to report that everyone's health has returned to normal. In addition, I now have an undiagnosed condition involving my brain stem that causes difficulty in speaking and walking at times. I have been going through testing, and I frequently require a wheelchair to get around.

The list goes on and on, but there is not a day that goes by that I don't laugh or find something good to smile about. Many people have asked how I have survived the various trials I have experienced and kept my marriage and faith intact. They wonder how I am still able to enjoy life and remain optimistic. Dr. Larry McCallum, one of my mentors, wrote this to me: "In many ways you've already lived more in your life than most 80 year olds." I do feel like that at times, especially right now, as I do not have complete control over my body. Just last night, Jim had to carry me across the room after my legs gave out.

But all credit for anything I am able to accomplish goes to God. Sometimes people think religion is the same as having a crutch. It's not. It's a personal relationship with the God of the universe who is still active in the world today.

> For we do not have a high priest who is unable to sympathize with our weaknesses, but we have one who has been tempted in every way, just as we are—yet was without sin.
> —Hebrews 4:15

Friends and family have certainly been there for prayer support and encouragement. I have also found strength in reading stories of survivors of the Holocaust. For many years now, I have studied about the ability of the human soul to triumph in horrific circumstances. I may have experienced more in my 40 years than some have in their 80 years, but those in the Holocaust suffered on a daily basis. And as I read their stories, I am encouraged.

I believe that I have gone through hardships not just for my own growth but also to sympathize with and, hopefully, to encourage others. It helps me to see the beauty in others and to embrace their differences. I think we all go through trials for these reasons. It's not uncommon to see people who have endured similar crises uniting together. We just sometimes need to be reminded that there is a purpose behind our suffering.

Lately, it seems that I am hearing from more and more people who are feeling numb, overwhelmed and exhausted. My e-mail is filled with prayer requests, and my heart breaks as I read how friends, family and even strangers are going through tough times. Yet I know there will be testimonies and that God is sufficient for their needs as well as mine.

I also receive many e-mails and calls from people who feel lonely and/or confused. Many suggest that this is because we live in a busy culture and high tech-impersonal society where communication is so available but a sense of true community is not being experienced. Many survivors of the Holocaust wrote about experiencing the silence of God. But in the process, they found community with each other and learned to wait on Him. They would question why things were happening, but in the midst of it all, they would see miracles or glimpse His mercy and grace. And this would sustain them for another day.

I pray that you find the same glimpses of His mercy and grace in your own daily struggles. Be encouraged, laugh often, and take a moment to hear the raindrops and see rainbows.

Jesus in Me

I am not powerful, but You empower my soul.
I am not beautiful, but You make me so.

So I fall to my knees in Your sanctuary
Giving all that is me, that You might cause me to be
The perfect thing that is all that You see
When You look and see Jesus in me

I am not wise or brave, but in You I believe.
I am not unafraid, but have You not sent me?

So I fall to my knees in Your sanctuary
Giving all that is me, that You might cause me to be
The perfect thing that is all that You see
When You look and see Jesus in me

I am not . . .
But You Are.

—John Hudgins